TASHRIH-UL-MOOSIQUI

TASHRIH-UL-MOOSIQUI

(Persian Translation of Tansen's Original Work 'Budh Prakash')

English Translation and Commentary by
Najma Perveen Ahmad

MANOHAR
2012

First published 2012

ISBN 978-81-7304-943-9

Published by
Ajay Kumar Jain *for*
Manohar Publishers & Distributors
4753/23 Ansari Road, Daryaganj
New Delhi 110002

Typeset by
Ajay Arts
New Delhi 110002

Printed by
Salasar Imaging Systems
Delhi 110035

To my grandchildren
Tarana, Kabir and Sahil

Contents

Acknowledgements

I was inspired to take up the research work, study and translation of important manuscripts on musicology by Professor (Mrs) Sumati Mutatkar, the former Dean, Faculty of Music and Fine Arts, University of Delhi. I wish to express my deep sense of gratitude for her enormous contribution to my learning and work in the field of music.

I have no words to express my indebtedness to my guru Ustad Naseer Ahmed Khan of the Delhi Gharana, whose guidance and blessings have greatly influenced me in acquiring deep insights and understanding the subtleties of music at every step.

I am highly thankful to Prof. S.A.H. Abidi, the renowned Persian scholar, who had been a constant source of inspiration for my work related to Persian manuscripts. I wish to acknowledge the contribution of Rahmatullah Farooqui Sahib for his dedicated help and support in the translation of this manuscript. My sincere thanks are due to Mrs. Chitra Santhangopal for the meticulous typing of this work.

I feel deeply indebted to my dear students and scholars, who have worked with me, for inspiring me with their queries, ideas and information. Their constant interactions with me have been a great source of insights, sense of joy and fulfilment.

Special thanks are due to Ms. Ghazala Amin for her help in taking up this work. I wish to acknowledge the support and patience of my husband Professor Abad Ahmad and all my family members who have been a great source of inspiration in completing this work. I wish to express my appreciation to Manohar Publishers & Distributors for their earnest efforts in bringing out this book in its present form.

University of Delhi
Delhi 110007

NAJMA PERVEEN AHMAD

Introduction and Historical Background

During the medieval period of Indian history, Hindustani music went through a process of transformation, synergistically absorbing the Arab, Persian and Central Asian influences that led to several scintillating and novel developments. There was also an intermingling of ideas and techniques in several other aesthetic fields. However, in music the synthesis of such influences was so profound that it would not be possible to delineate the Indian and foreign elements.

Hindustani music that developed as a result of such interaction is essentially based on the rich Indian heritage, its deeply embedded traditions and their refinement through beautifully blending the external influences.

Music was patronized and thrived at the imperial courts and at the centres of provincial kingdoms during the Mughal period. As is well known, among all the emperors of Mughal dynasty, the reign of Akbar (AD 1556-1605) stands out as a golden era for the patronage and development of music and fine arts. Akbar's period has been immortalized by a number of great musicians like Tansen.

Abul Fazl in *Ain-e-Akbari* testifies to the fond attention given by the emperor to music, and the patronage extended by him to the musicians. Akbar's fondness for music is vividly described by Abul Fazl:

> His majesty pays much attention to music, and is the patron of all who practice this enchanting art. There are numerous musicians at the court—Hindus, Iranis, Turanis, Kashmiris, both men and women. The court musicians are arranged in seven divisions—one for each day in the week. When His Majesty orders, they let the wind of harmony flow, and thus increase intoxication in some and sobriety in others.

During this period the well-known Ragas, such as Darbari Kanhra, Mian Ki Todi, Mian Malhar, and Mian Ki Sarang were innovated. These Ragas are attributed to Tansen, who was included among the nine gems of Akbar's court.

Tansen's birth is ascribed to the prayer and blessings of Sheikh Mohammad Ghaus. It is believed that when he was five years' old, his father brought him to the Sheikh. Since then Tansen lived with him. According to I.A. Arshi ('*Hindustan Ke Chand Mashhoor Moosiqar*', *Aaaj Kal*, 1956): "Tansen was deeply impressed by the compositions of Nayak Bakshoo and he decided to learn the art of music. After the death of Mohammad Ghaus he went to Daulat Khan, the son of Sher Shah." Later he moved over to Raja Ramchandra Baghela of Rewa, where he was highly honoured. Tansen's fame impressed Emperor Akbar so much that he persuaded the Raja to send him to his court. Tansen lived at Akbar's court with great honour and respect. He died in the year AD 1580.

Emperor Akbar realized that the main reason for hostility between the Hindus and Muslims was their ignorance of each other's religion and culture. Therefore, under his instructions, a large number of translations were undertaken of works on various subjects—both religious and secular. With the result that a considerable number of standard works on music, both in original and translations from Sanskrit were undertaken. Apart from educating the readers about the various aspects of music, the writers during this time were also motivated by the spirit to preserve the rich heritage of Indian Music as contained in the Sanskrit works, and to make it available to future generations of musicians and musicologists.

The earliest known Persian writings on Indian music are *Ghunyat-ul-Munya* (AD 1374) and *Lahjat-e-Sikandar Shahi* (Lodi period—AD 1414-1526). The only one copy of *Ghunyat-ul-Munya*, written in Gujarat in 1374-5, is known to exist in India Office Library in London. It was translated in English and published by Prof. Shahab Sarmadi in 2003. It is based on Sanskrit works, some of which are no longer available. *Lahjat-e-Sikandar Shahi* was written in the fifteenth century under the patronage of Khawas Khan and was dedicated to Sultan Sikandar Lodi. This work has been edited and published in its Persian form by Dr. Syeda Bilqis Fatema Husseini. Among the known manuscripts in Indian musicology a reference is often made about the works of Tansen. The three works which are generally attributed to him are—*Sangeetsar, Raag Sagar* and *Raagmala.*

Some scholars have often mentioned about the manuscript of *Sangeetsar* in their writings. I have obtained some information regarding this manuscript from Pt. Balkrishan, son of Pt. Gopal Singh, *Pakhawaj* player of Gwalior, who possessed some parts of it. In this work the author has mentioned about the three branches of music—*Geet, Vadya* and *Nritya.* He has also described *Moorchhana* and the classification of Ragas.

A description of the musical instruments prevalent during that period has also been narrated in this work.

Another work that is attributed to Tansen is *Raag Sagar* which is written in Persian language. Its contents are more or less similar to *Sangeetsar.* The manuscript expounds musical terms like *Gram, Moorchhana,* along with the classification of Ragas. Surprisingly there is no mention of Tansen as its author. The Indira Gandhi National Centre for Arts, New Delhi, has a microfilm from original manuscript that is preserved at Jama Masjid Trust, Bombay.

A manuscript attributed to Tansen with the title *Raagmala* is available in some manuscript libraries of India and abroad. There is no sufficient evidence to establish the fact that it was authored by Tansen. Besides, there is a reliably proven Sanskrit work entitled *Raagmala* written by Pt. Pundrik Vitthal in the year AD 1516. Several copies of this work are available in various manuscripts' libraries and archives. It was first published in the year AD 1914 by Nirnaya Sagar Press, Bombay. Further a revised edition of Pundrik Vitthal's works—*Sadrag Chandrodaya, Raagmala, Raag Manjari* and *Nartan Nirnaya* was edited by Shri R. Satyanarayana along with its translation and commentary. It was published in a single volume entitled *Pundrikmala* by Sangeet Nritya Academy, Bangalore, Karnataka in the year AD 1986.

Today when we have entered into the new century, it would be most appropriate to pay attention to all those musicians and scholars who have given a lot to the subject of music and provided numerous manuscripts to the world of music, which are shining like jewels in the field of musicology. These works are written in Sanskrit, Hindi, Persian, Urdu and other local Indian languages, which have been preserved in the form of books and manuscripts.

The modern Indian musicologists do realize the importance and need of studying the Persian and Urdu works. Pt. V.N. Bhatkhande, the most outstanding Indian musicologist, has repeatedly referred in his works to the need for examining Persian literature on Indian music. This is because of the fact that most of these sources contain translations and references from ancient Sanskrit texts, which either were destroyed and are not now available, or could not be preserved on account of political instability and other reasons of that period. Therefore, the knowledge of these precious works can only be derived from the Persian and Urdu manuscripts.

When I was pursuing my doctoral research work entitled 'Development of Hindustani Music during Seventeenth and Eighteenth Centuries, with special reference to Persian and Urdu Works', I met late Prof. Nurul Hasan Ansari of the Department of Persian, University of Delhi. He was the author of *Farsi Adab ba Ahd-e-Aurangzeb* (1969). This book is an authentic work on Persian manuscripts written during Aurangzeb's rule. While discussing with him about Persian manuscripts on Indian musicology, he informed me that a Persian manuscript entitled *Tashrih-ul-Moosiqui* is a translation of *Budh Prakash*, a work authored by Tansen.* He also mentioned that the only copy of this work is available in the Shirani collection of Punjab University Library, Lahore.

Ever since I came to know about this work, I was curious to study it and examine whether there was an evidence of

* In the author's opinion the title *Bodh Prakash* seems more appropriate than *Budh Prakash*. However, since the author of Persian manuscript Hakeem Arzani has clearly written it as *Budh Prakash* (p. 3), and Prof. N.H. Ansari has also described it as *Budh Prakash* in his work cited above (p. 460), therefore to ensure authenticity in translation, the title *Budh Prakash* has been retained.

it being an authentic translation of Tansen's work *Budh Prakash*. I felt that probably like *Man Kautuhal*, of which only Persian translation *Raag Darpan* is available, so also *Budh Prakash* may be available only in the translated form. I was informed by a few academics that a microfilm copy of *Tashrih-ul-Moosiqui* was acquired by some scholars at the University of Delhi. However, my efforts to obtain this microfilm copy were in vain, as it was not traceable.

Although there were many constraints in acquiring a copy of this work, fortunately later I was able to have an access to a photocopy version of *Tashrih-ul-Moosiqui* through some well-wishers and music lovers.

On examining this manuscript, I found a clear mention of Tansen as author of *Budh Prakash*, which has been translated by Mohammad Akbar urf Mohammad Arzani son of Mohammad Muqeem. According to Dr. N.H. Ansari (*Farsi Adab ba Ahd-e-Aurangzeb*, p. 460), Mohd. Arzani was a well-known Hakeem (Unani Physician), and had written a number of books on medicine, probably during the period of Aurangzeb. The description on page 3 of the manuscript clearly verifies the authorship of this work by Tansen, though there is no mention of the language in which it was written.

Through this work, it is my modest endeavour to present before the world of music an English translation of *Tashrih-ul-Moosiqui*, with the hope that it will bring to light the work of great musician Tansen, which he recorded in his treatise entitled *Budh Prakash*. In addition to the translation of this work, I have also attempted to present brief commentary and my observations wherever required.

Preface to the Manuscript *Tashrih-ul-Moosiqui*

In the preface to the manuscript the author has expressed gratitude and appreciation for the blessings of 'Allah' the God Almighty, Prophet Mohammad and all the ancestors who have inspired him to undertake this work. In his words:

> The majesty of God Almighty is so great that no human being can ever describe it in words. All admiration is for Allah who inspired the hearts and souls of the elder musicians to recite music by the grace of *La-Ilaha-Illallah* (God is one and there is no god except Him). All salutations to the Prophet and his progeny, who was chosen by God to guide us to follow the virtuous path in life.

Following it, the author has quoted Arabic couplets in admiration of Allah, Prophet Mohammad and the elder musicians.

The author has mentioned his name as Mohammad Akbar urf Mohammad Arzani, son of Mohammad Hakeem. According to him the knowledge of the art of music is very complex and difficult to describe and explain. He states:

The art of music is intricate and difficult to explain. Therefore, I decided to translate the work of Meer Tansen, *Budh Prakash*. I have translated this work in Persian in a summarized form, and given it the title: *Tashrih-ul-Moosiqui*.

The book is based on eight 'Baabs' (chapters):

1. First Baab – The Origin of Music
2. Second Baab – The Types of *Samaah*
3. Third Baab – Description of *Svara* (Musical Notes) and Attributes of Musicians
4. Fourth Baab – Principles of Ragas, Their Roots and Offsprings (Raga, Raaginees, Putras and Bharyas)
5. Fifth Baab – Classification of Ragas
6. Sixth Baab – The Time Theory for the Performance of Various Ragas
7. Seventh Baab – The Description of 'Milonis' (Innovating Mishra Ragas by Combining Different Ragas)
8. Eighth Baab – Musical Instruments and the Tala System

FIRST BAAB
The Origin of Music

In this chapter the author has described several legends associated with the origin of the word *Moosiqui* (the music). He points out that there are divergent viewpoints regarding the origin of music:

One viewpoint associates the origin of music with the legend of Prophet Moses. According to this belief, Prophet Moses found a unique stone in the river Nile and was advised by angel Gabriel to keep it carefully for the future. Later when he was wandering with his followers in the wilderness, he came to a desert where there was no water. Seeing the plight and suffering of the entire community because of heat and thirst, he prayed to God for relief by providing water. Then he was inspired by the God Almighty to strike the stone with his staff (the stick) that led to the gushing forth of several springs of fresh water. Seeing this miracle, his followers collectively started reciting *Moosa-fi-Haqqui*. The rhythm of their recitation repeatedly is believed to be the origin of the term *Moosiqui* (the music).

Another legend attributes the origin of music with Prophet Mohammad's ascendance to heaven and the dialogue on his return with Hazrat Ali, his son-in-law who was known for his unparalleled bravery and courage. Prophet Mohammad shared the secrets of nature and God's creation which were bestowed on him. Hazrat Ali pleaded with the Prophet that he will not be able to retain these secrets because of their enormous magnitude. He was advised by the Prophet to unburden himself of these secrets in some far-off deserted and dried well, away from the population. When Hazrat Ali found such a well and followed the instruction, the well was miraculously revived and fresh water began to overflow all around. All the creatures in its vicinity were intoxicated by drinking the water and in that condition started reciting melodious songs. These voices continued even after the bodies of the animals were no more and had turned into dried skins and twines. The passers-by were amazed by the musical sounds all around and spontaneously recited the following couplet:

Khushk taar-o khushk chob-o khushk post
Az kuja mi aayad een awaaz dost

Although the wood, the skin and the strings are dry, O my friend, where does this sonorous musical sound come from?

Surprisingly apart from the description given of the above-mentioned two legends regarding the origin of music, the author of the book has not described several commonly believed viewpoints of other writers of Sanskrit and Persian manuscripts. In these works names of various gods, goddesses, *Rishis* and *Munis*, etc., have been mentioned as the originators of music, such as—Shiva, Parvati, Sarasvati, Hanuman, Narad, Tumburu, Kohal, Kashyap, Atotra, Bharat, Shardul, Ha-Ha, Hu-Hu, Vayu, and Disha, etc.

Further the author has described Gwalior as the main centre of music, which attracted a great number of musicians (vocalists and instrumentalists) of that period. In his opinion most of the fundamental knowledge and guiding principles of music (Hindustani Music) emanated from Gwalior.

An important and noteworthy information that has been highlighted in this work is about an outstanding musician of that period—Madhvamal, who has been described as the only person who could challenge the musicians of Gwalior. He was an unparalleled talented artiste of his time, who was gifted with an enormously forceful voice, the effects of which have been described in glowing terms.

Another highly significant information has been cited in the manuscript about a *Risala* (Treatise written by Madhvamal Brahmin under the title: *Aprampaar Mahan Bharat*). This work has been considered as one of the most authoritative and unique works on the fundamental principles and tenets of musicology. Now a question that arises regarding the above-mentioned statements in the manuscript is: Whether the person cited here as an extra-ordinary musician and his work refer to the well-known Bharat and his treatise *Natyashastra*, or does it refer to a distinct and different person about whom the other works are silent?

The author proceeds to describe the two eminent musicians of the period—Tansen and Baiju. At some places he has addressed Tansen as Meer Sahib and Baiju as Birju. In his opinion Tansen excels Baiju Bawra in singing Raag Deepak. By quoting the opinion of his contemporary scholars and impartial critics, the author has expressed the opinion that Tansen and his *ustad* (guru) had complete mastery of singing Raag Deepak and they could create a thrilling atmosphere through this Raga that no musician could match. He has also given a vivid account of rendering this Raga with the analogy of a bird called *Quqnus* (Phoenix), which is consumed by the fiery Raga and is reborn. In order to learn this Raga and witness for himself the transformation of the bird like a phoenix, Tansen sought the help of Hazrat Mohammad Ghaus Gwaliori. The author also mentions that under the influence of Hazrat Mohammad Ghaus he chose to convert his religion to Islam.

Following this the author has given an elaborate account of an episode when several leading musicians such as Baiju, Surat Khan, Bilas Khan, Chand Khan and Ramdas, etc., had assembled in the court of Emperor Akbar. The author states:

> They were debating different aspects of music in accordance with the directions of the emperor. Each one of them claimed supremacy over Tansen. When the issue got prolonged the musicians challenged that if Meer Sahib through his performance of Raag Deepak can light the candles and water filled lamps, they would all become his disciples. Meer Tansen took up the challenge and was able to demonstrate his prowess, and consequently all musicians accepted his supremacy and the emperor rewarded him with robes of honour.

SECOND BAAB
Types of *Samaah*

This chapter deals with the four types of *Samaah*. In this context the author has given the following four versions of music which represent the facets of music from different points of view:

1. *Haraam* (Prohibited)
2. *Makrooh* (Contemptible)
3. *Mubah* (Proper)
4. *Mandoob* (Pleasing or desirable).

1. *Samaah* is evil for those persons who become engrossed with worldly desire and passion and whose thoughts and feelings get inclined toward bad conduct by listening to *Samaah*.
2. Music is contemptible or undesirable for those who treat it lightly and casually without appreciating its intricacies.
3. *Samaah* is proper for those who appreciate its aesthetic beauty and find pleasure in the sweet voice of the vocalists and sounds of musical instruments. Music does not evoke evil thoughts in the minds of such people.
4. *Mandoob* (desirable) has been described in the context of Sufi music. It liberates the mind from worldly

bondages, enables movement towards spiritualism and search for truth.

At this point the author has referred a book entitled *Kitab-e-Dastoorul-Quzaat* written by Imam Ghazaali. According to him, the listening and practice of *Samaah* is spiritual duty of everyone. Further, he concludes that listening of *Samaah* is preferable for those who have transcended desires and whose hearts are cheerful.

At the end of the chapter the author has referred to a religious *Fatwa* (edict) pronounced by some contemporary priests who prohibited listening to a few musical instruments like *Mazamir* (Psaltery) in the *Samaah*, because in his opinion, such instruments are mostly played in the musical gatherings of alcoholics.

THIRD BAAB

Description of *Svara* and Attributes of Musicians

The third chapter begins with the description of the seven *svaras* namely *Kharaj* (*Shadaj*), *Rikhab* (*Rishabh*), *Gandhar*, *Madhyam*, *Pancham*, *Dhaiwat* and *Nikhad* (*Nishad*).

In his opinion it is essential for a musician to have thorough understanding and full command in singing these *svaras*, because they are the foundation on which the entire edifice of music depends. In this context a word *Istarana* has been mentioned (but its description is vague and ambiguous). Further the author states that the first six *svaras* have originated from the melodious sounds produced by various birds except the seventh *svara*, i.e. *Nishad*, whose origin has been associated with *Airawat* (the mythological elephant). In Persian it has been described as a white elephant, and in Arabic it is called *Feel-e-Mahmood*.

It may be noted that whereas the author in the above description has attributed the origin of six *svaras* to the sounds produced by the birds and only one *svara* to an animal, most of the renowned musicologists of Sanskrit treatises have described only four *svaras* to the sounds of birds (peacock, *chatak*, *kraunch*, and *kokila*) and the remaining three to the sounds produced by other animals (goat, frog, and elephant). For example, Matanga, the author of *Brihaddeshi* has associated the origin of seven *svaras* to the imitation of the following sounds in a Sanskrit *shloka* as translated below:

> The peacock speaks Shadaja, the Chataka (bird) speaks Rishabha; the goat speaks Gandhara, the Kraunch (Bird) speaks Madhyama in the Pushpasadharana time (spring); Kokila speaks Panchama in the rainy season; Dardura (frog) speaks Dhaivata. O Devi ! in the same way the elephant always speaks Nishada. (See *Brihaddeshi* of Matanga, ed. Dr. Premlata Sharma, IGNCA, 1962).

ATTRIBUTES OF THE MUSICIANS

According to the book, it is important for the vocalists to follow the ten essential *usools* (fundamental principles) and avoid the ten undesirable attributes. The defects of musicians have been classified in two categories:

(a) The defects based on incompetence of a musician.
(b) The defects based on the deficiencies in the voice and unnatural behaviour while performing.

Following have been identified in the first category:

1. *Be-Taal-Tarannum*
2. *Be-Taan Naghma*
3. *Be-Aalaap Sarood*

In the second category seven defects of a vocalist have been described as follows:

1. The voice of the vocalist is similar to the sound produced by crow.
2. To have a scowl on the forehead.
3. To shake the neck frequently while singing.

4. To turn the face towards both the shoulders.
5. Instability in rendering the notes.
6. Singing through nasal sound.
7. Shaking the whole body at the time of performance.

As we know, almost all the Sanskrit and Persian treatises have discussed the subject of the characteristics of musicians in detail. For example, Mirza Khan the author of *Tohfatul Hind* (a treatise written during the seventeenth century) described them as follows:

CHARACTERISTICS OF MUSICIANS

1) Mrisht, (2) Madhur, (3) Chehal, (4) Tristhan, (5) Sukhavah, (6) Komal, (7) Shravuk, (8) Karuna, (9) Ghat, (10) Snigdh, (11) Gaarh, (12) Slakshana, (13) Prachur, (14) Raktiyukt.

DEFECTS OF MUSICIANS

(1) Sandisht, (2) Uddhrisht, (3) Bhet, (4) Shankit, (5) Kampit, (6) Karali, (7) Kaagi, (8) Kapil, (9) Betal, (10) Karabh, (11) Uddand, (12) Jhombak, (13) Vakri, (14) Prasari, (15) Nimilak, (16) Apsvar, (17) Veras, (18) Avyavasthit, (19) Avyakt, (20) Sthanbhrasht, (21) Anavdhan, (22) Sutkari, (23) Saannunasik, (24) Karkash.

Keeping in view the above description, two points are worthy to be noted: Firstly, the author of *Tashrih-ul-Moosiqui* described only the negative qualities of vocalists and avoided the positive characteristics of a good musician. Secondly, he has not consulted any other Sanskrit work of that period, and probably he has only translated those descriptions which were available in Tansen's work *Budh Prakah.*

FOURTH BAAB
Principles of Ragas, Their Roots and Offsprings

(RAAG, RAAGINEE, PUTRA AND BHARYA)

This is a comprehensive chapter, which covers a detailed classification of the Ragas and their sub-categories. The author has elaborated the Raag-Raaginee classification system, giving vivid description of their special characteristics. In the words of the author:

> I wish to make it clear to the readers that in the opinion of the knowledgeable musicians, the entire system of Indian music is based on six main Ragas, and its thirty branches are called Raaginees. Each Raga has eight sub-categories which have been named as their sons. Following are the six basic Ragas:
>
> 1. Raag Bhairav
> 2. Raag Malkauns
> 3. Raag Hindol
> 4. Raag Deepak
> 5. Sarpraag (also called as Shri Raag)
> 6. Raag Megh.
>
> It is interesting to note that the author has ascribed the

origin of Ragas to some prophets, angels, divine names quoted in Quran and other mythological beliefs as given below:

1. Raag Bhairav has been associated with Prophet Dawood.
2. Raag Malkauns has been associated with Gibrael.
3. Raag Hindol is attributed to Rizwan (the custodian of the Paradise).
4. Raag Deepak has been associated with the sounds and noises at the time of sunrise.
5. Shree Raag has been associated with the sound of *Azdaha* (the mythological python who is believed to support the earth).
6. Raag Megh has been associated with the thunder of cloud during rainy season.

Following is a brief description of the Ragas as elaborated by the author, which is more or less similar to the description of Ragmala in the other texts of Persian and Sanskrit works belonging to that period. The author has only described the verbal image of six basic Ragas, unlike others, who have also dealt with the description of the Raaginees, their Putras, and Bharyas (sons and daughters-in-law).

Raag Bhairav: A handsome male dressed in white, sitting on an ox or seated on carpet of deer skin, wearing a necklace of human skulls, golden bangles in both hands, and whose forehead is shining like the full moon.

Raag Malkauns: An intelligent healthy male of wheatish complexion, who is wearing a black-coloured scented dress and pearl necklace. He is seated on an elevated platform surrounded by beautiful women. Describing the sweetness of this Raga, the author has also written a Persian couplet.

Raag Hindol: A young handsome male having a playful temperament, dressed in yellow colour robes, wearing a crown on his head, and seated on a swing. He posseses a sweet voice.

Raag Deepak: A strong and mighty male dressed in red robes riding an elephant and wearing a pink red-coloured coral necklace. In the author's view the impact of this Raga is so strong that the spark of the sound of rendering this Raga can light a flame of fire that can burn the musician like a moth is burnt by the candle light.

Sarp Raag: A handsome saint looking male who has long hair, wearing a necklace of fine polished beads, and holding a lotus flower in his hand.

Raag Megh: A brave male, whose voice resembles the roar of a lion, who looks like a king and sometimes appears as a fierce looking person in rage. He is dressed in yellow and wears a crown on his head, holding a flower and is accompanied by beautiful women. One distinctive characteristic of its extreme expression is that it can catalyze the clouds and cause a rainfall.

DESCRIPTION OF RAAGINEES

According to the author, each Raga has five Raaginees. They are classified in the following manner:

Raaginees of Raag Bhairav

1. Bhairavi
2. Abheri
3. Madhmadhvi
4. Saindhvi
5. Bengali

Raaginees of Raag Malkauns

1. Todi
2. Dhanashri
3. Gunkali
4. Khambhvati
5. Dhaulshri

Raaginees of Raag Hindol

1. Ramkali
2. Devsakh
3. Lalit
4. Bilawali
5. Patmanjari

Raaginees of Raag Deepak

1. Desi
2. Kamodini
3. Kedari
4. Nat
5. Kamod

Raginees of Sarpraag (Raag Shree)

1. Malshri
2. Maru
3. Gauri
4. Dhanashri
5. Asawari

Raaginees of Raag Megh

1. Tunk
2. Gujri
3. Bhopali

4. Deshkar
5. Malshri

Regarding the definition and descriptions of above-mentioned Ragas, the author is of the view that among the musicians of his period there were differences of opinion. He has given the description of the Ragas and Raaginees after consulting the maestros of the art of music of his time, in addition to translating it from the original manuscript of Tansen's work. Further, he has described the *Putras* (sons) of basic Ragas. Each Raga has been ascribed eight Putras. Thus the total number of Putras are forty-eight. A list of such Ragas is given below:

Name of Ragas	*Names of Putras*
1. Raag Bhairav	(1) Karpancham, (2) Harsha, (3) Desavar, (4) Bengal, (5) Madh, (6) Madhav, (7) Karnavati, (8) Mangla Bilawal.
2. Raag Malkauns	(1) Virag Maru, (2) Mewad, (3) Sabhti Mishrang (not clear), (4) Barwa, (5) Chandrikasheesh, (6) Sorath, (7) Raaj Bhramra, (8) Nanda.
3. Raag Hindol	(1) Mangal Ishtak, (2) Tikachandra, (3) Chanchal, (4) Phool Nand, (5) Pota (not clear), (6) Bhakhar, (7) Vardhan (8) Basanta.
4. Raag Deepak	(1) Bhanwar Kalyan, (2) Kamal, (3) Ram, (4) Katol (not clear), (5) Karan, (6) Kamodha, (7) Champak, (8) Himal.

5. Sarp Raag (Shree)	(1) Mali Gaura, (2) Saranga, (3) Svaramak (4) Dev Gandhar, (5) Shritunk, (6) Baadar Gound, (7) Nagbhavuk (not clear), (8) Aheera.
6. Raag Megh	(1) Kanhra, (2) Sarang, (3) Kedara, (4) Jaldhar, (5) Gajdhar, (6) Gandhar, (7) Baghar Pandh (not clear), (8) Sankara-Bharan.

The author describes that there was difference of opinion in the names of the sons of Ragas, but he had tried to write about the widely accepted opinion. He has also mentioned about the *Bharyas* (wives of the sons). However, detailed description of such Ragas is missing. Further, he has mentioned about one hundred and fifty-two popular Ragas which were innovated by combining different Ragas. The names of such Ragas are given below:

Bilawal, Basant, Basanti, Lalit, Laliti, Sarang, Malhar, Poorva, Poorbi, Bheem, Palaas, Tribhinna, Jaini (not clear), Maru, Gaura, Shyam, Kamod, Kalyan, Bhakh, Khamaj, Paraj, Jaijaiwanti, Sorath, Bhankhar, Bhatiyar, Vibhas, Desika, Asaa, Sinduri, Gaud, Aiman, Aimani, Ghara, Jogawati, Askandi, Kedari, Bahar, Kauns, Parchha (not clear), Kedara, Trivin, Desavali, Lachari, Sikhri, Husseini, Pilu, Birahni, Adana, Shahana, Sughrai, Bangali, Desri, Manjhak, Bhavi, Barhans, Parchhamra (not clear), Jait Sarang, Deepaki, Mangali, Heenar, Heenri (not clear), Dev Gandhar, Kukubh, Saakh, Kaali, Hindoli, Kanosia, Nagar, Bhakhi, Suha, Palas, Ansaa, Dhol, Sorath, Karlawati, Khat, Ghareeq, Gujri, Pradeepika, Dekdhari (not clear), Motiki, Tilang, Bheem, Chikari, Sorthi, Khambhavati, Sankari,

Bhakhi, Chuck, Parchaba (not clear), Natoda, Bheemi, Jhoomri, Kandhari, Askanda, Khamaji, Bhawti, Gaudki, Ramee, Bihari, Lajwanti, Soorji, Waganjoti (not clear), Saraswati, Palashri, Gunkali, Jati, Lankdahan, Gauran (not clear), Malwa, Kandhar, Barari, Naunaat, Parai, Deskala, Saurastrak, Sawantak, Nagsoha, Rajhans, Kolahal, Chitrola, Deskali, Lalhawati (not clear), Trivin, Tunk, Bhola Raag (not clear), Surdang, Shyam, Kumbhi, Sankaraman (not clear), Bagesri, Bhairavi, Bhakhi, Chakia, Parai, Gaurkali, Sundari, Kandaki, Kandhari, Kola (not clear), Kharam (not clear), Saleekha (not clear), Lobha, Jaijaiwanti, Kalyani, Bansi, Harni.

It may be noted here that although the author of the Persian manuscript has mentioned the number of these Ragas as 152, the actual number of Ragas quoted in the manuscript is only 150. Two Ragas, viz., Bilawala and Lalliti mentioned in the manuscript, have not been found in any other writing of that time or earlier period. The author has described Lalliti as the third Raginee of Raag Hindol. These two ragas have not been included in the above-mentioned list of ragas.

FIFTH BAAB
Classification of Ragas

The classification of Ragas has been an integral part of musicology since early times. Different musicologists have followed varied approaches in classifying the Ragas. This chapter of the manuscript has been devoted to the classification of Ragas and their further sub-classifications. In addition to translating the Ragas as discussed in *Budh Prakash*, the author has also elaborated some of the most prevalent and contemporary Ragas of his time. A noteworthy aspect of this chapter is that it contains information of various Ragas in addition to those which have been described in Tansen's *Budh Prakash*. This is a very significant and informative part of the work. The Ragas have been classified by the author as follows:

(i) Bhairava Shuddha
(ii) Kaneri
(iii) Kural
(iv) Sankha Sankeerna

Each of the above-mentioned Ragas has been associated with one *Kali* (flower bud). Here the metaphor of flower bud has been utilized, further these four types have been mentioned as daughters of Raag Bhairav.

Following are the four *Kalis* of Raag Bhairav:

1. Gunkali
2. Ramkali
3. Sankeerna Kali
4. Prakash Kali

In addition, the following seven *Raaginees* have been described:

1. Todi—It is the first Raaginee of Malkauns.
2. Patmanjari—It is the fifth Raaginee of Hindol.
3. Nat—It is the fifth Raaginee of Deepak.
4. Malshri—It is the first Raaginee of Shri Raag.
5. Gauri—It is the second Raaginee of Shri Raag.
6. Asavari—It is the fifth Raaginee of Shri Raag.
7. Gujri—It is the second Raaginee of Raag Megh.

Varieties of Todi

1. Shuddha Todi
2. Berari Todi
3. Bahaduri Todi
4. Desi Todi
5. Jaunpuri Todi
6. Asavari Todi
7. Mangali Todi
8. Lachari Todi
9. Pinaki Todi
10. Khat Todi (it is different from Khat Tanseni)

Varieties of Patmanjari

1. Tanseni Patmanjari
2. Soordasi Patmanjari

Varieties of Nat

1. Nat Shuddha

2. Nat Kedaru
3. Nat
4. Nat Malhar
5. Nat Narayan
6. Nat Ahiri
7. Nat Asawari

Varieties of Malshri

1. Shri Shuddha
2. Jait Shri
3. Pratap Shri
4. Dhaulshri

Varieties of Gauri

1. Shuddha Gauri
2. Jaiti Gauri

Varieties of Asawari

1. Shuddha Asawari
2. Jogiya Asawari
3. Asawari Surat Khan

Varieties of Gujri

1. Shuddha Gujri
2. Khat gujri
3. Shyam Gujri

Names of the Sons and Their Wives of Ragas

(1) Bilawal, (2) Lalit, (3) Saakh, (4) Sarang, (5) Malhar, (6) Poorba, (7) Gaura, (8) Jog, (9) Shyam, (10) Kamod, (11) Kalyan, (12) Kanhra, (13) Bhakh, (14) Kedara, (15) Sankara, (16) Khamaj, (17) Paraj, (18) Jaijaiwanti, (19) Sorath.

Varieties of Bilawal

1. Shuddha Bilawal
2. Kukubh Bilawal
3. Shukla Bilawal
4. Alhaiya Bilawal
5. Khamaj Bilawal
6. Jaijaiwanti Bilawal
7. Shankara Bilawal
8. Kuchcheli Bilawal (not clear)
9. Aiman Bilawal
10. Kamodi Bilawal
11. Madhur Rasia Bilawal
12. Sakhia Bilawal
13. Bhakh Bilawal
14. Suha Bilawal

Varieties of Lalit

1. Lalit
2. Lalita Kedaru
3. Lalit Maru
4. Lalliti

Varieties of Saakh

1. Devsakh
2. Gunsakh
3. Lachcha Sakh
4. Bhanwar Sakh

Varieties of Sarang

1. Shuddha Sarang
2. Brindavani Sarang
3. Barhans Sarang
4. Milarmoon Sarang

5. Sawant Sarang
6. Dhuria Sarang
7. Sorath Sarang
8. Sujanak Sarang
9. Madhumad Sarang
10. Kopalhari Sarang
11. Nahari Sarang

Varieties of Malhar

1. Shuddha Malhar
2. Gaud Malhar
3. Dhuria Malhar
4. Milarmoon Malhar (not clear)
5. Ramdasi Malhar
6. Soordasi Malhar
7. Sawant Malhar
8. Asawari Malhar
9. Meghawali Malhar
10. Basanti Malhar
11. Hindoli Malhar

Varieties of Poorva

1. Shuddha
2. Puriya Dhanashri
3. Poorva Vibhas
4. Poorvi Kalyan

Varieties of Gaura

1. Shuddha Gaura
2. Mali Gaura
3. Chati Gaura
4. Shri Gaura

Varieties of Jog

1. Shuddha Jog
2. Mangli Jog

Varieties of Shyam

1. Shuddha Shyam
2. Shyam Kalyan
3. Kedara Shyam

Varieties of Kamod

1. Kamod
2. Tilak Kamod
3. Sawant Kamod

Varieties of Kalyan

1. Shuddha Kalyan
2. Aiman Kalyan
3. Yaman Kalyan
4. Bhopali Kalyan
5. Poorva Kalyan
6. Vipar Kalyan (not clear)
7. Shyam Kalyan
8. Sanwarin Kalyan
9. Kamod Kalyan
10. Nat Kalyan
11. Bheem Kalyan
12. Khem Kalyan

Varieties of Kanhra

1. Shuddha Kanhra
2. Nayki Kanhra
3. Shahana Kanhra
4. Adana Kanhra
5. Sughrai Kanhra

6. Akel Kanhra (not clear)
7. Mandarekh Kanhra
8. Bagesri Kanhra
9. Kanoosia Kanhra
10. Basanti Kanhra
11. Khamaji Kanhra
12. Sorath Kanhra
13. Jaijaiwnti Kanhra
14. Darbari Kanhra
15. Karnati Kanhra
16. Ghara Kanhra
17. Mangalikh Kanhra
18. Daulati Kanhra

Varieties of Bhakh

1. Shuddha Bhakh
2. Bhakhra

Varieties of Kedara

1. Shuddha Kedara
2. Shyam Kedara
3. Nat Kedara
4. Lalita Kedara
5. Maru Kedara

Varieties of Sankara

1. Shuddha Sankara
2. Sankarabharan
3. Sankara Sankeerna
4. Sankarasan

Varieties of Khamaj

1. Shuddh Khamaj

2. Parajiya Khamaj

Varieties of Paraj

1. Paraj
2. Jogia Paraj

Varieties of Jaijaiwanti

1. Shuddha Jaijaiwanti
2. Jaijaiwanti Kanhra

Varieties of Sorath

1. Shuddha Sorath
2. Sarang Sorath

SIXTH BAAB

The Time Theory for the Performance of Various Ragas

This chapter of the manuscript deals with the concept of relating various Ragas to different times of the day and changing seasons.

In the words of the author:

> The learned and knowledgeable maestros of music emphasize the importance of keeping in mind the timing of performance of various Ragas and Raginees to the disciples and the practitioners of music. They advise and instruct their disciples and practitioners to follow the time framework of Ragas of different hours.

At a later point in the manuscript, the author has mentioned that performance of Ragas at wrong times may cause ill effects on one's health and lead to serious consequences. To support this belief, a couplet also has been quoted.

In addition to the timings of the different Ragas, the author has also given an account of the relationship between the six main Ragas (Bhairav, Malkauns, Hindol, Deepak, Shree and Megh), and associated them with the six seasons of the year. It may be noted that this classification is similar to the Persian system of *Maqamat*. These are also consonant with the position of sun and Zodiac signs. The author of the manuscript has explicated this classification as follows:

Name of the Raga	*Time*
Bhairav	The last hours of the night, that blend with the dawn.
Malkauns	From midnight to sunrise.
Hindol	From beginning of the sunrise till the first quarter of the day.
Deepak	Between the first quarter and the midday.
Shree Raag	Between the third quarter of the day and the sunset.
Megh	From midday until the dusk and any time during rainy season.
Bhairavi	From sunrise to midday.
Abheri, Madhmadhvi, Saindhvi and Bangali	During the first part of the morning.
Todi and Dhanashri	After the first quarter in the forenoon.
Dhaulshri	Between the third quarter of the day and the sunset.
Gunkali	Between the last part of the night and before the forenoon.
Khambhavati	Midnight.
Devsakh	After the passage of the first quarter of the day.
Lalit	Early forenoon till the sunset.

Bilawali	From sunrise to late forenoon.
Patmanjari	From midday until sunset.
Desi	Forenoon.
Kamodini	From the first part of the night until mid-night.
Kedari	Same as for Kamodini.
Nat	Before the sunset until mid-night.
Maru	From mid-night to the passage of three quarters of night.
Gauri	From the third part of the day until the sunset.
Dhanashri Huseini	From early to late forenoon.
Asawari	From sunrise to the first quarter of the day.
Antak or tunk (not clear)	From first quarter of the day to mid-day.
Gujri	From early part of the night until early forenoon.
Bhopali	From early hours of night until around mid-night.
Poorva	From the passage of first quarter of the day till before sunset.
Chandrikasheesh	From the first part of the night till midnight.
Sorath	From midnight to midday.
Mangal Ishtak	From the first quarter till mid-night.
Tikachandra and Chanchal	No clear indication.

Bhakhar, Drohan, Pota and Basanta	From past mid-night till the third quarter of night.
Bhanwar Kalyan, Donal, Katola and Kram	From the beginning of night until past a quarter of the night.
Kamodha	Same as for Bhakhar.
Himala	From beginning of the morning till past a quarter of the day.
Mali Gaura	A little before afternoon until the sunset.
Panchak	The author has not identified any specific time in the manuscript.
Surang	Mid-night
Dev Gandhar	From past mid-night to little after the sunrise.
Shree Tunk	From afternoon until the sunset.
Tukbhanutak (not clear)	Mid-night.
Aheera	Same time as for Bengal.
Dhurant and Jalandhar	Same time as for Bengal (the description of Raag Bengal is missing).
Kedara	From forenoon till late afternoon.
Gajdhar	Same time as for Kanhra.
Suhab and Bakharnodha (not clear)	From the late morning until before noon.
Sankarabharan	Same as for Bhakhar (i.e. from mid-night till the third quarter of night).

Bilawal	After the mid-night until the third quarter of night.
Basant, Pancham, Lalit and Sakhan	Same as for Asawari.
Sarang	From forenoon until before sunset.
Malhar	From forenoon until late afternoon and any time during rainy season.
Kalyan	From the first quarter of the night until midnight.
Khamaj and Kedara	From forenoon till late afternoon.
Paraj	From midnight till the later half of the night.
Jaijaiwanti	From first part of the night until few hours before the dawn.
Sorath and Bakhia	Same as for Jaijaiwanti.
Bhatiyar	From sunrise to the early forenoon.
Vibhas	After the third quarter of night until the sunrise.
Deshkar	Same as for Vibhas.

From the above-stated account of the timings for the various Ragas, it is evident that the author of the manuscript has not covered the full range of Ragas. In his words:

> There are a number of opinions and viewpoints regarding the timings for the performnace of particular Ragas. An attempt to cover all the viewpoints would have led to confusion and distraction. I have, therefore, selected only those Ragas which are widely known and popular among the musicians. I hope that I would not be misunderstood

and will be forgiven for my selectivity by the readers of this book.

SIX SEASONS AND THEIR RAGAS

In addition to the timings of the different Ragas, as stated above, the author has also given an account of the relationship between the six main Ragas and associated them with the six seasons of the year. It may be noted that this classification is similar to the Arabian and Persian system of *Maqamat* which are also associated with the position of sun and Zodiac signs. The author of the manuscript has elaborated this classification as follows:

Name of the Raga	*Persian Names of the Months Associated with the Raga*
1. Raag Bhairav	Shahriwar and Mehar
2. Raag Malkauns	Dae and Bahman
3. Raag Hindol	Isfandar and Farwardi
4. Raag Deepak	Urdi Bihisht and Khurdad
5. Raag Shree	Abaan and Azar
6. Raag Megh	Teer and Murdad

It is noteworthy that several other Persian and Sanskrit works of that period have given similar classifications by relating the Ragas with the Indian names of the months and seasons. For example, Faqueerullah, author of the *Raag Darpan* (seventeenth century) has described the classification as follows:

Name of the Ragas	*Month*	*Season*
Raag Hindol, its Raaginees and Putras	Chaitra-Vaisakh	Basant

Raag Deepak, its Raaginees and Putras	Jaishth-Asarh	Greeshm
Raag Megh	Sawan-Bhadon	Pawas
Raag Shree	Kuar-Kartik	Sheet
Raag Malkauns	Aghan-Poos	Hemant
Raag Bhairav	Magh-Falgun	Shishir

A critical analysis of this chapter reveals that the author has not covered the entire range of Ragas as expounded in the other known works of musicology of his period. He has been selective and has justified his choice to avoid the controversy, because of different viewpoints about the time theory of Ragas. Further, he has specified the timings in minute details. In order to interpret these details, an attempt has been made in this translation to simplify the approximate timings and relate them to the generally accepted framework of time-theory.

SEVENTH BAAB

Description of *Milonis*: Combination of Ragas

The author has used the word *Miloni* for combination of Ragas, in place of the well-known terms like—Chhayalag, Sankeerna and Mishra Ragas, used by the authors of other works of the period. This is the most significant and comprehensive chapter of the manuscript. Its uniqueness is that it covers the classification system of the wide range of well-known Ragas mentioned in *Budh Prakash*, which has some different nuances as compared to the description given in Persian works of later medieval period.

The chapter has been divided in the following five sections:

1. Description of the *Milonis* of the six main Ragas.
2. Description of the *Milonis* of the thirty Raaginees.
3. Description of the *Milonis* of the sons of six Ragas.
4. Description of the *Milonis* of sons and their wives of six Ragas.
5. Description of some other *Milonis*.

COMBINATION OF VARIOUS RAGAS

1. Raag Bhairav — It is considered Shuddha Raag which has been formed without any combination.

2. Raag Hindol	Combination of Raag Basant, Poorvi, Kalyan and Kamod.
3. Raag Deepak	Combination of Lajwanti Soorji and Aganjyoti.
4. Shri Raag	Combination of Gauri, Atang (not clear) and Barhans.
5. Raag Megh	Combination of Lalit, Bhairav, Pancham and Poorba. It is also called as Megh Malhar.
6. Raag Malkauns	Combination of Parchia, Bihari and Hindoli.

DESCRIPTION OF THE *MILONIS* OF THIRTY *RAAGINEES*

Raaginees of Bhairav

1. Bhairavi	Combination of Bhairav, Kandhar, and Todi.
2. Ahiri	Combination of Motki, Shyam, Malhar and Ramkali.
3. Madhmadhvi	Combination of Asavari, and Saindhvi.
4. Saindhvi	Combination of Asavari and Sorath.
5. Bangali	Combination of Berari, Gauri, Gujri.

Raaginees of Malkauns

1. Todi	Combination of Lalit, Dhanashri, Shuddha Shyam, Bhairav and Bhairavi.
2. Dhanashri	Combination of Parai (not clear) Devsakh and Bheem. In this context Raag Husseini also has

	been mentioned which has been earlier described as the fourth Raaginee of Shri Raag.
3. Dhaulshri	Combination of Berari and Jaitshri.
4. Gunkali	Combination of Gaun or Gaund and Adana.
5. Khambhavati	Combination of Chaskari (not clear) Khamaj and Malhar.

Raaginees of Hindol

1. Ramkali	Combination of Bheem, Palashri, and Lalit.
2. Devsakh	Combination of Sankarabharan, Kanhra, and Malhar.
3. Lalit	Combination of Vibhas, Desi and Shade of Pancham.
4. Bilawali	Combination of Kamodi, Kalyan and Bilawal.
5. Pat Manjari	It is of two types: (1) Tanseni, (2) Nayaki. Tanseni is a combination of Poorvi, Poorva, Bhakh, Dhanashri and Gauri; and Nayaki is the combination of Maru, Dhaulshri, Dhanashri, and Khumbi.

Raaginees of Deepak

1. Desi	Combination of Dhaulshri, Gaura, Todi and Khat.
2. Kamodhni	Combination of Sughrai Kanhra, and Sorath.
3. Kamodi	Combination of Nat Kalyan, and Malhar.

4. Kedari	Combination of Sankri, Shyam and Malshri.
5. Nat	Combination of Lankadahan, Madhumadhvi, Bilawal and Sankarabharan.

Raaginees of Shri Raag

1. Malshri	Combination of Madhumadhvi, Sursati, Kedara and Sankarabharan.
2. Bhakha	Combination of Bhakhi, Jag-parachiya (not clear), Natwa and Shyam.
3. Gauri	Combination of Poorvi, Barhans, Bihari, and Jati.
4. Dhanashri Husseini	Combination of Khat, Desi, and Bheemi.
5. Bangali	Combination of Kanhra, Khamaj, Shyam, Bhairav, and Basanti.

NAMES OF PUTRAS (SONS) OF MAIN RAGAS AND THEIR MILONIS

Following is the description of the names of *Putras* of main Ragas and the combination of different Ragas:

Putras of Bhairav

Surprisingly, the number of eight Putras of Raag Bhairav have been mentioned but the description of first, second, third and fourth Putras are missing.

5. Madh	Combination of Manjhak and Bhairav.
6. Madhav	Combination of Kanhra, Shyam, and Bhairav.

7. Karanmadhvi	Combination of trifle of Bilawal, Laliti and Bhairav.
8. Mangla Bilawal	Combination of Vaig Andhar, (may be Dev Gandhar), Bilawal and Bhairav.

Putras of Raag Malkauns

1. Virag Maru	Combination of Paraj, Kedari, and Malkauns.
2. Sabodh	Combination of Bahar, Malhar, and Malkauns.
3. Santhi Mishrang	Combination of Anoddha and Malkauns (not clear).
4. Barwa	Combination of Piloo, Dhanashri, trifle of Todi, Bhawi and Malkauns.
5. Chandrikashesh	Combination of Aimani and Malkauns.
6. Sorath	Combination of Barhans, Sorath, Sarang, Malkauns.
7. Rajbhramara	Combination of Parchhamra (not clear) and Malkauns.
8. Nanda	Combination of Chait and Malkauns.

Putras of Raag Hindol

1. Mangal Ishtak	Combination of Malshri, Kalyan, Shyam, Kedara, Hindol.
2. Tikachand	Combination of Lalit Malhar and Hindol.
3. Chanchal	Combination of Bhairami (not clear), Bilawal, Basant and Hindol.

4. Phoolmanand (not clear)	Combination of Sarangi, Malhari, and Hindol.
5. Bhabhakhar	Combination of Sankara, Deepki, Bilawal, and Hindol.
6. Bardhan	Combination of Basanti, Nagar, and Hindol.
7. Pota	Combination of Mangli, Kanhra and Hindol.
8. Basanta	Combination of Kanhra, Basant, triffle of Bhairav and Hindol.

Putras of Raag Deepak

1. Bhanwar Kalyan	Combination of Marwa, Kalyan, Jaiti, Vibhas.
2. Donal	Combination of Deepki and Dhanashri.
3. Ram	Combination of Barhansi and Sarang.
4. Kanwla or Khatola	Combination of Kanhra and Laliti.
5. Kram	Combination of Bilawal, Aiman and Hampari or Hanpari.
6. Panchak	Combination of Dhanashri, Sorath, Barhans, Basant, Bangla.
7. Kamodho	Combination of Sorath, Kanhra and Kamod.
8. Himala	Combination of Malhar and Vaig (In the author's view Vaig or Vaig Adhar is the name of the same Raga. At some places it has been spelt as Devgandhar also.

Putras of Shree Raag

1. Mali Gaura	Combination of Bhairav, Nat, Kalyan, Malhar, Devgandhar and Gauri.
2. Saranga	Combination of Shuddha Sarang Barhans Sarang and Sorath.
3. Surang	Combination of Suha and Malhar.
4. Dev Gandhar	Combination of Aasi, Dhol, Bhairav and Sarang.
5. Sri Nag	Combination of Gauri and Jait (in the opinion of the auhor this is the most appropriate Raga in the context of Samah music).
6. Baadar Gaud (not clear)	Combination of Adana and Malhar.
7. Nagbhanook (not clear)	Combination of Barwa and Laliti.
8. Ahira	Combination of Nat, Bilawal, Gaud Malhar and Khamaj.

Putras of Raag Megh

1. Kanhra	Combination of Kalika, Malhar, and Bilawal.
2. Dhurant	Combination of Kamod, Basant, Nat and Syam.
3. Kedara	Combination of Baraj (perhaps Paraj) Hindolu, Kaunsia or Kausumbh and triffle of Bhakh.
4. Jalandhar	Combination of Nat, Syam and Sorath.
5. Tajdhar (not clear)	Combination of Ghara, Gaund, Malhar, and Basant.

6. Sohab (not clear)	Combination of Sakhri and Malhar.
7. Pagharnodha (not clear)	Combination of Todi, Lalit and Basant.
8. Sankarabharan	Combination of Malshri, Kedara, Basant, Shyam and Bhaki.

DESCRIPTION OF THE PROGENY OF PUTRAS AND BHARYAS (SONS AND THEIR WIVES) OF RAGAS

1. Basant Pancham	Combination of Basanti Kanhra, Kedari, Bahar, Kanoos, Lalit and Bhairav.

(Here the author states that according to another opinion, this Raga is the combination of Sarang, Nat, Malhar, Bilawal and Devgiri. In his view this was the popular opinion among the musicians of his time.)

2. Bhakhra	Combination of Kedara, Gauri, and Shyam.
3. Khamaj	Combination of Malshri and Malhar.
4. Vibhas	Combination of Bhakha, Rami and Bhopali.
5. Sawantak	Combination of Nat, Kedara, Kanhra, Kamod and Shyam.
6. Malhar	Combination of Nat, Sarang and Megh.
7. Deskar	Combination of Gauri, Maru, Dhaulshri, Jaitshri and Dhanashri.
8. Aiman	Combination of Kalyan, Kedara and Bilawal.
9. Devgiri	Combination of Shuddha Sarang and Poorvi.
10. Barhans	Combination of Gauri and Vibhas.

11.	Sarang	Combination of Devgiri, Malhar, Nat and Shuddha Nat.
12.	Hamper or Hanpar (not clear)	Combination of Deskali, Kalyan, Gujri, and Shyam.
13.	Kukubh	Combination of Bilawal, Poorbi, Kedara, Devgiri and Madhu-madhvi.
14.	Devgandhar	Combination of Gauri, Shuddha Sanwari, Sarang and Bhairav.
15.	Gaura	Combination of Gauri, Nat and Hamper (not clear).
16.	Suha	Combination of Shuddha Bilawal and Bageshri.
17.	Lankdahan	Combination of Pahari and Kedara.
18.	Khatraag	Combination of Asawari, Todi, Shyam, Malwa, Kandhar and Berari.
19.	Deshkala	Combination of Desi, Todi and Lalit.
20.	Jaurastrak (not clear)	Combination of Asawari, Poorvi, Bhairav and Dev Gandhar.
21.	Naagsoha	Combination of Suha, Malhar and Kedara.
22.	Rajhans	Combination of Shri Raag and Malwa.
23.	Kolahal	Combination of Kalyan, Bhakhra and Kanhra.
24.	Chitraphoola	Combination of Ramkali, Gujri, Deskali and Basant.
25.	Sankraman	Combination of Lankadahan, Sorath and Bilawal.

26. Parai	Combination of Deskar, Todi and Trivin.
27. Gaudkali	Combination of Gujri and Asawari.
28. Navnaat	There are four opinions about the combination of Ragas in this Raga. 1. Combination of Kalyan and Nat. 2. Combination of Kanhra and Nat 3. Combination of Kamod and Nat. 4. Combination of Sarang and Nat.
29. Parai	This Raga is written twice. One has been already mentioned above. According to second opinion it is a combination of Devgiri, Poorvi and Gauri.
30. Poorvi	Combination of Jogiya, triffle of Devgiri and Poorva.
31. Poorva	Combination of Dhaulshri and Kanhra.
32. Bheem	Combination of Dhanashri, Barwa and Kanhra.
33. Trivin	Combination of Marwa, Gauri, Dhanashri, and least appearance of Gaura.
34. Jaitishri	Combination of Malkauns, Marwa, Poorva and Gauri.
35. Marwa	Combination of Vibhas, least appearance of Gauri and Maru.

According to the author of the manuscript:

I have given the above description of whatever information was available on the basis of thorough study. I have consulted the well-known contemporary scholars and musicians to ensure that the information is complete and authentic, so that I may not be accused and condemned for laxity in my work.

DESCRIPTION OF SOME OTHER COMBINATIONS

The author of the manuscript has described four verieties of Raag Bhairav:

1. Bhairav Shuddha: It cannot be combined with any other Raga.
2. Combination of Bhairav and Sankarai.
3. Combination of Bhairav and Karlawati.
4. Combination of Bhairav and Lalit.

Gunkali	Combination of Dev Gandhar, Bhairav, and Basanti.
Ramkali	Combination of Bhairav, Gujri and Desi Todi.
Prakashkali	Combination of Bilawal and Bhairav.

Varieties of Todi

1. Shuddha Todi	It cannot be combined with any other Raga.
2. Barati Todi	Combination of Deskar, Trivin and Todi.
3. Bahaduri Todi	Combination of Todi, trifle of Shree, and Desavli.
4. Desi Todi	Combination of Asawari, Todi and trifle of Lachari.
5. Jaunpuri Todi	Combination of Barwa, Todi, and trifle of Malhar.
6. Asawari Todi	Combination of Asawari and Todi.
7. Manglik Todi	Combination of Sughrai, Todi and trifle of Bilawal.

8. Lachari Todi	Combination of Dhanashri, Desi and Husseini.
9. Pinaki Todi	Combination is missing.
10. Khat Todi	Combination is missing.

Varieties of Nat

1. Shuddha Nat	It cannot be combined with any other Raga.
2. Nat Kedaru	No description has been given.
3. Nat Malhar	No description has been given.
4. Nat Narayan	Combination of Nat, Malhar, Bilawal and Adana.
5. Nat Ahiri	Combination of Nat, Bilawal, Sorath and Bhakh.
6. Nat Maru	Combination of Nat and Maru.
7. Nat Asawari	Combination of Sakhri, Malhar and Nat.

Varieties of Malshri

1. Shuddha Malshri	It cannot be combined with any other Raga.
2. Jaitshri	Combination of Jait, Dhanashri and Gauri.
3. Pratapshri	Combination of Shyam, Gauri and Dhanashri.
4. Dhaulshri	Description is not given.

Varieties of Gauri

1. Shuddha Gauri	It cannot be combined with any other Raga.
2. Chaiti (not clear)	Combination of Malkauns, Maru, Poorva and Gauri.

Varieties of Asawari

1. Shuddha Asawari	It cannot be combined with any other Raga.

2. Jogiya Asawari	Combination of Jogawati, Asawari, trifle of Todi, Askandki and Desi.
3. Asawari Surat Khan	Combination of Asawari, Barwa and trifle of Todi.

Varieties of Gujri

1. Shuddha Gujri	It cannot be combined with any other Raga.
2. Khat Gujri	Combination of Khat, Ramkali and Gujri.
3. Shyam Gujri	Combination of Gujri, Shyam, and Bilawal.

Varieties of Bilawal

1. Shuddha Bilawal	It cannot be combined with any other Raga.
2. Kukubh Bilawal	Combination of least appearance of Malshri and Jaijaiwanti.
3. Shukla Bilawal	Combination of Gaud and Nat.
4. Alhaiya Bilawal	Combination of Bilawal, Bhakh, Bhopali and Poorva.
5. Khamaji Bilawal	Combination of Khamaj, Bilawal.
6. Jaijaiwanti Bilawal	Combination of Bilawal and Jaijaiwanti.
7. Sankar Bilawal	Combination of Bilawal and Sankar.
8. Kachchbali Bilawal	Combination of Ghara, Malhar and Bilawal.
9. Aiman Bilawal	Combination of Aiman Kalyan, and Bilawal.
10. Kamodi Bilawal	Combination of Kamodi and Bilawal (according to another

	opinion it is called Devgiri Bilawal).
11. Madhur Rasiya Bilawal	Combination of Bhakh and Bilawal.
12. Sakhiya Bilawal	Combination of Kanhra, Malhar and Bilawal.
13. Bhakh Bilawal	Combination of Bhakh and Bilawal (same as Madhur Rasiya Bilawal).
14. Suha Bilawal	Combination of Suha and Bilawal.

Varieties of Lalit

1. Lalit Bahar	Combination of Parajia, Bahar, Kedara and Lalit.
2. Lalit Kedara	Combination of Kedar and Lalit.
3. Lalit Marwa	Combination of Marwa and Lalit.
4. Lalliti	Combination of Lalit, Bhairav and least appearance of Bahar.

Varieties of Sakh

1. Devsakh	Combination of Adana, Todi, Sukhrai and Malhar.
2. Gunsakh	Combination of Shahana, Malhar and Gaund.
3. Lachchasakh	Combination of Sukhravi, Malhari and Asawari.
4. Bhanwarsakh	Combination of Kanhra, Bilawal and Malhar.

Varieties of Sarang

1. Shuddha Sarang	It cannot be combined with any other Raga.

2. Brindavani Sarang	Combination of Sarang, Barwa and Malhar.
3. Gaud Sarang	Combination of the trifle of Devgiri, Poorva Kalyan and Sarang.
4. Madhumad Sarang	Combination of Sorath, Malhar, Sarang, Adana and Barhans.
5. Barhans Sarang	Combination of Sarang and Barhans.
6. Malarhoon Sarang (not clear)	Combination of Sarang, trifle of Gaud and least appearance of Sorath.
7. Gobarhari Sarang	Combination of Sarang, Poorva, Kalyan and Devgiri.
8. Sawant Sarang	Combination of Malhar, Sarang and Bilawal.
9. Dhuria Sarang	Combination of Lalit, Sarang and Malhar.
10. Sorath Sarang	Combination of Sorath and Sarang.
11. Sujanak Sarang	Combination of Khamaj, Malhar and Sarang.

Varieties of Malhar

1. Shuddha Malhar	It cannot be combined with any other Raga.
2. Gaud Malhar	Combination of Adana, Suhi and Malhar.
3. Megh Malhar	Combination of Lalit, Bhairav, Pancham and Poorva.
4. Dhuriya Malhar	Combination of least appearance

	of Lalit, Kanhra Shahana, Sarang, Khamaj and Malhar.
5. Malarhoon Malhar	Combination of Adana, Khamaj and Malhar.
6. Ramdasi Malhar	Combination of Barwa, Sorath, Jaijaiwanti Sarang and Malhar.
7. Soordasi Malhar	Combination of Barhans, Malhar, triffle of Kanhra and least appearance of Sarang.
8. Sawant Malhar	Combination of Barwa, Nat and Malhar.
9. Sawani Malhar	Combination and Dev Gandhar and Malhar.
10. Meghawali Malhar	Combination of Jaijaiwanti, Sarang, Gaud and Malhar.
11. Hindoli Malhar	Combination of Malhar, triffle of Bahar, and Lalit.

Varieties of Gaura

1. Shuddha Gaura	It cannot be combined with any other Raga.
2. Mali Gaura	Combination of Bhairav, Natu, Malshri, and Dev Gandhar.
3. Jaiti Gaura	Combination of Jait and Gaura.
4. Shree Gaura	Combination of Gauri, Dhanashri and Trivin.

Varieties of Jog

1. Shuddha Jog	It cannot be combined with any other Raga.
2. Jog Sankali	Combination of triffle of Poorvi, Dhaul, Barwa and Asa.

Varieties of Shyam

1. Shuddha Shyam	It cannot be combined with any other Raga.
2. Shyam Kalyan	Combination of Kalyan, Bilawal and Kedara.
3. Shyam Kedara	Combination of Shyam and Kedara.

Varieties of Kamod

1. Shuddha Kamod	Combination of Malhar and Kalyan (according to another opinion it is a combination of Bilawal and Kamod).
2. Tilak Kamod	Combination of Khat and Kamod.
3. Sawant Kamod	Combination of Sawant and Kamod.

Varieties of Kalyan

1. Shuddha Kalyan	It cannot be combined with any other Raga.
2. Aiman Kalyan	Combination of trifle of Bilawal, Poorva, Kalyan and Dhaul.
3. Yaman Kalyan	Combination of Poorbi, Bhakh, Kanhra and Ghara.
4. Bhopali Kalyan	Combination of Vibhas, Pahari, and Kalyan.
5. Poorba Kalyan	Combination of Poorva, Kalyan and Bhakh.
6. Hamper Kalyan (not clear)	Combination of Hamper, Natu, and Bhopali Kalyan.
7. Shyam Kalyan	Combination of Shyam and Kalyan.

8. Sawni Kalyan	Combination of Nat, Bhopali, Bhakh, Kedara and Kalyan.
9. Kamod Kalyan	Combination of Nat, Kalyan, Gaud and Bilawal (according to some musicians it is the combination of only Kamod and Kalyan).
10. Nat Kalyan	Combination of Nat and Kalyan.
11. Bhakh Kalyan	Combination of Bhakh and Kalyan.
12. Bheem Kalyan	Combination of Kalyan, Kamodi, Bilawal and Kedara.
13. Khem Kalyan	Combination of Nat, Sorath, Humper (not clear) and Kalyan.

Varieties of Kanhra

1. Shuddha Kanhra	No combination.
2. Nayaki Kanhra	Combination of Malhar, trifle of Paraj, Sukhravi or Sughrai and Kanhra.
3. Shahana Kanhra	Combination of Ghareeq, Jaijaiwanti and Kanhra.
4. Adana Kanhra	Combination of Gaud Malhar and Kanhra.
5. Sukhravi Kanhra	Combination of Devsakh, least appearance of Kanhra and Malhar.
6. Akel Kanhra	Combination of Pradeepki Jhoomri, Kanhra and Sankara.
7. Mandrekh Kanhra	Combination of Kanhra, Barwa, Malkauns and Malhar.
8. Bageshri Kanhra	Combination of Kanhra and Malshri.

9. Kaunsia Kanhra	Combination of Malkauns and Kanhra.
10. Basanti Kanhra	Combination of Bahar, Basant and Kanhra.
11. Khamaji Kanhra	Combination of Khamaj and Kanhra.
12. Sorath Kanhra	Combination of Sorath and Kanhra.
13. Jaijaiwanti Kanhra	Combination of Jaijaiwanti and Kanhra.
14. Darbari Kanhra	Combination of Devsakh, Adana, Malkauns, Kanhra and Malhar.
15. Karnati Kanhra	Combination of Kanhra, Maru, Sorath and Poorvi.
16. Ghara Kanhra	Combination of Tilangi, Kanhra, Khamaj and Bhakh.
17. Mangaleek Kanhra	Combination of Kanhra and Kukubh Bilawal.
18. Daulti Kanhra	Combination of Malkauns, Dhanashri and Kanhra.

Varieties of Bhakh

1. Shuddha Bhakh	It cannot be combined with any other Raga.
2. Bhakhra	Combination of Nat, Bilawal, Dhanashri and Bhakh.

Varieties of Kedara

1. Shuddha Kedara	It cannot be combined with any other Raga.
2. Shyam Kedara	Combination of Shyam and Kedara.

3. Nat Kedara	Combination of Nat and Kedara.
4. Lalita Kedara	Combination of Lalit, Kedara, and Malkauns.
5. Maru Kedara	Combination of Maru, Paraj and Kedara.

Varieties of Sankara

1. Shuddha Sankara	No combination.
2. Sankarabharan	Combination of Malshri, Kedara, Basant, Shyam and Bhakhi.
3. Sankara Arun	Combination of Sankara, Kedara and Dhanashri.
4. Sankara Sankeerna	Combination of Sankara and Paraj.

Varieties of Khamaj

1. Shuddha Khamaj	No combination.
2. Jogiya Khamaj	Combination of Jog and Paraj.

Varieties of Jaijaiwanti

1. Jaijaiwanti	Combination of Barhans, Sorath, Sarang and Malhar.
2. Jaijaiwanti Kanhra	Combination of Jaijaiwanti and Kanhra.

Varieties of Sorath

1. Shuddha Sorath	No combination.
2. Sorath Sarang	Combination of Sorath and Sarang.

At the end of this chapter the author has discussed about *Raag Sagar.* According to him, explication of six and thirty Raaginees are known as *Raag Sagar* (the ocean of Ragas). Probably the author is hinting at the book *Raag Sagar*, which is attributed to Tansen.

EIGHTH BAAB

Description of Musical Instruments and the Talas

This chapter gives an account of the various musical instruments and enumeration of Talas. It is relatively a brief and sketchy description of these subjects, whereas they have been dealt with and elaborated in much greter detail and depth in other Sanskrit and Persian works on Indian musicology. Only the names of various instruments and Talas have been mentioned in the manuscript without giving any further details.

Given below are the names of the twelve musical instruments that have been identified in the manuscript:

1. Tamboor
2. Been
3. Rebab
4. Mridang
5. Ud
6. Jal Tarang
7. Daira
8. Dholak
9. Pakhawaj
10. Burdi or Pardi
11. Qanun
12. Kheru

Similarly the names of Talas have been mentioned as follows:

1. Yakka
2. Chahar Taal
3. Dutala
4. Adda Taal
5. Soornath
6. Sawari Panj Taal
7. Sawari Haft Taal
8. Dhamar (also known as Bhakh)
9. Kabitt
10. Bramh Yazda Taal
11. Bramh Taal
12. Bramh Nooh Taal
13. Dhruvak
14. Math Taal
15. Roodang
16. Dastan
17. Fardost or Farodast

Although the author has given the number of Talas as nineteen, only seventeen Talas have been identified in the manuscript.

Taal, an important element of Indian classical music, has been discussed in detail by most of the authors of Sanskrit and Persian treatises. Bharat and Dattila have mentioned the *Margi* Talas. In *Sangeet Makrand* five *Margi* Talas have been described. The names of the five *Margi* Talas discussed in various treatises are: *Chanchatputa, Chachputa, Shatpitaputrak, Sampadveshtika* and *Udghatta.* In the opinion of Nanyadev, each of these five *Margi* Talas has hundreds of varieties.

Generally *Desi* Talas are said to be one hundred and eight in number, inclusive of five *Margi* Talas. In *Sangeet Makrand*

and *Sangeet Samaysar* one hundred and one Talas have been identified. *Sangeet Ratnakar* mentions one hundred and twenty *Desi Talas*. It is noteworthy that some other important Persian manuscripts of the author's contemporary period have identified different number of Talas. For example, the author of *Usulun-Naghmat-e-Asifi* has described only nine Talas which were popularly practised during his period. But in *Tohfatul-Hind* as many as ninety-two Talas have been identified as given below:

(1) Kokila, (2) Raj Vidha Dhar, (3) Jaimahak, (4) Tikamod, (5) Vijayanand, (6) Krida, (7) Jaishri, (8) Makrand, (9) Krivitt, (10) Shri Krivitt, (11) Bhadra Mali, (12) Sam Taal, (13) Nandan, (14) Mathka, (15) Bamathka, (16) Visham Taal, (17) Uday Taal, (18) Dhendki, (19) Visham Taal, (20) Mall Taal, (21) Purna Kangal, (22) Khand Kangal, (23) Sam Kangal, (24) Visham Kangal, (25) Aidwan, (26) Chitra, (27) Jhamp Taal, (28) Abhang, (29) Basant, (30) Pratap Shikhar, (31) Jai Jhampal, (32) Chitramukh, (33) Madan, (34) Rat Taal, (35) Parvati Lochan, (36) Leela, (37) Karna Taal, (38) Lalit, (39) Raj Narayan, (40) Lakshmi Ish Taal, (41) Lalit Priya, (42) Shree Nand, (43) Janak, (44) Pradhan, (45) Raag Pradhan, (46) Khat Taal, (47) Antar Krida, (48) Bilokat Taal, (49) Gaj Taal, (50) Baran Jat Taal, (51) Hans, (52) Karana, (53) Saras Taal, (54) Chhand, (55) Chandrakala, (56) Amiya Taal, (57) Shikhand, (58) Ugra Tali Taal or Rudra Tali Taal, (59) Mohna, (60) Dand Taal, (61) Kumand Taal, (62) Kovid Taal, (63) Kuldheen Taal, (64) Gauri Taal, (65) Raj Nirgang, (66) Raj Mardand, (67) Nishank, (68) Sarangdev, (69) Ektali, (70) Gandak, (71) Matth Vritta, (72) Nishank Leela, (73) Bramha Taal, (74) Vichitra, (75) Lubdha Taal, (76) Rupak, (77) Isht Taal, (78) Shankh, (79) Prati Taal,

(80) Sunj Taal, (81) Sanmukh Trital, (82) Ishtalika, (83) Gaund, (84) Anang Taal, (85) Abinand, (86) Raihaiko (not clear), (87) Karogi, (88) Varna Mukh Taal, (89) Nayandi, (90) Davanal, (91) Bhagna, (92) Sursati Abhran.

From the foregoing description it is evident—as mentioned in the beginning of the chapter—that the author of the manuscript, Mohammad Akbar urf Mohammad Arzani has not gone into depth in studying and narrating the contemporary musical instruments and Talas. He has emphasized in the manuscript at several places that he was not a musician or musicologist. Therefore, he has admitted his inability to cover the various aspects of the subject comprehensively. This leads to the plausible inference that the translated manuscript does not fully cover the original version of *Budh Prakash*.

It also emerges from a close analysis of the translated manuscript that it has a greater focus on the practising aspects of classical music, unlike the other manuscripts of that period, which have a greater emphasis on the Shastrik (theoretical) contents of the subject. Because of this orientation of the manuscript, I have attempted to give comparative literature and information from the other Persian and Sanskrit works in the commentary along with the translation.

Another significant point that is highlighted by a close examination of *Tashrih-ul-Moosiqui* is that its style and content strongly reflect the approach of a practising musician, rather than of a scholarly musicologist. Consequently, the proposition that *Budh Prakash* is an authentic work written by Tansen is further confirmed.

References

Ansari, N.H., *Farsi Adab ba-Ahde-Aurangzeb*, Indo-Persian Society, Delhi, 1969.

Ansari, N.H. (ed.) *Tohfatul-Hind* (Persian manuscript by Mirza Khan), Vol. I, published in Iran by Bunyad Farhang-e-Iran, 1950.

Arshi, I. A., *Hindustan Ke Chand Moosiqar* (Urdu), Aaj Kal, Publications Division, Patiala House, New Delhi, 1956.

Blochman and Jarret, *Ain-e-Akbari* (English translation), Vol. 1, Calcutta, 1883.

Matanga, *Brihaddeshi*, et. Premlala Sharma, IGNCA, 1962.

Raag Darpan, Persian manuscript by Faquirullah, Dr. Zakir Husain Library, Jamia Millia Islamia, New Delhi.

Sarmadi, Shahab (ed.), *Ghunyatul Munya* (Persian manuscript), Asia Publishing House Private Ltd., New Delhi, 1971.

Usul-un Naghmat-e-Asifi, Persian manuscript by Ghulam Raza-bin-Mohammad Panah, Dr. Zakir Husain Library, Jamia Millia Islamia, New Delhi.

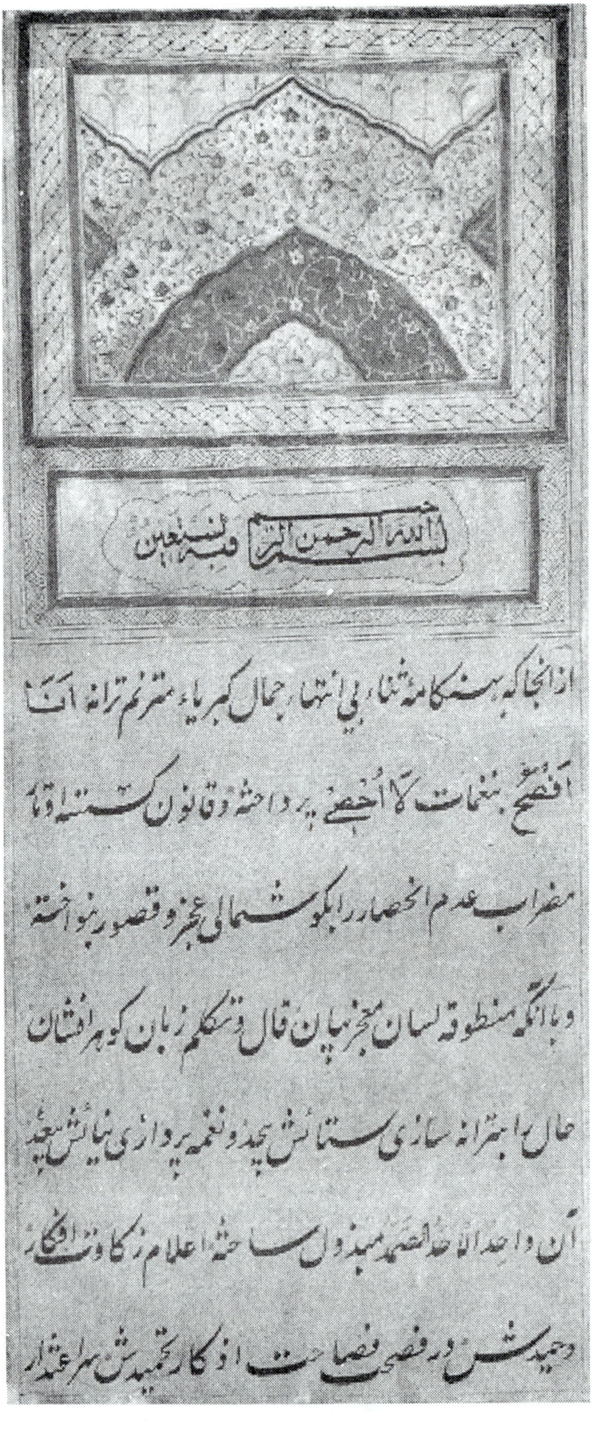

بسم الله الرحمن الرحیم و به نستعین

از انجا که بسی کامه ثنای بی انتهای جمال کبریای مترنم ترانه انا
افصح بنغمات لا احصی پرداخته و قانون گسسته تارها
مضراب عدم انحصار را بگوشمال عجز و قصور نواخته
و با انکه منطوقه لسان معجز بیان قال و متکلم زبان گوهر افشان
حال را بترانه سازی ستایش بیحد و نغمه پردازی نیایش بیعد
آن واحد الاحد الصمد مبذول ساخته اعلام زکاوت افکار
وحیدش در فصحی فصاحت اذکار تحمیدش سر اعتذار

و تارک اقتصار مانند چنگ فرو انداخته زبان قاصر بیان

این هیچمدان را چه یارا که بمجلس نشاط و محفل انبساط انعام

خاص و عام بشکرانه آن یگانه جل جلاله و عم نواله ترنمی

آغاز دارد اما بمقتضای لازم الاداء امر جلیل القدر مفهومه کلام

خیر الانام علیه و آله الصلوة و السلام بتمهید تحمید آن وحید

می پردازد الحمد لمن جعل قلوب الواصلین

مترنما بذکر لا اله الا الله و ارواحهم

مغنیا بنغمة لا اله سواه و الصلوة و السلام

علی سیدنا محمد الذی اصطفاه و علی کل

واحد من آله و صحبه الذی اهداه بیت

ساقی ز شراب شوق سرمست کردان ٭ مستانه درند و می پرستم کردان

یک جرعهٔ جام بیخودی نوشانم ... فارغ ز خیال نیست و هستم گردان

اما بعد پس میگوید ذره اصغر محمد اکبر المعروف به محمد ارزانی

ابن مقبول بارگاه کریم محمد مقیم که چون انکشاف حجاب

و گشود نقاب از چهر مهر سپهر راز سراپا ناز محبوبه و مطلوبه

نازک مزاج ابتهاج امتزاج موجب ناشکیبائی و باعث

دلربائی سعید و شقی موسومه بعلم موسیقی بنابر وقت کلام

در وقت پیام زبان درافشان و دلاله رساله موصوفه معروفه

مسمیه بدو پر کاس درین تصنیف لطیف آفتاب برج

حقیقت گوهر درج طریقت مطلع انوار الهی منبع اسرار

کماهی زبده کونین میر تانسین قدس سره در عشق عاشق

صادق نزاکت سمع ظل اللهی و قدام مجلس جاودق لطافت طبع

بادشاهی دام ظلاله و اجلاله بتحریر و ترقیم ترجمه فرخنده و آمال خلاصة الکمال

بحصول رسید لحمدالله الاجابه این سراپا انکسار در هنگام سعادت و

التیام از جهة مهارت تمام و تجربت تمام اندرین فن بتحریر

و تسطیر ترجمه موصوفه بامور امر اقتضا قدر کرد و بعد لیس

من بعد کتابیش مشتمل ساخت بر هشت باب و بتسمیه اش

تشریح الموسیقی پرداخت و الیه المرجع و المآب

باب اول در بیان منشا و مبدا علم و تسمیه موسیقی

باب دوم در بیان انواع سماع باب سیوم در بیان

لوازمات و موافقات مغنی باب چهارم در بیان تعداد

اصول و فروع و اثمار شجره علم موصوف باب پنجم در بیان

تقسیم بعض اصول و فروع و اثمار شجره مذکوره باب ششم در بیان اوقات

سرائیدن اصول و فروع و بعض اشعار مذکوره باب هفتم در بیان انبیا یعنی

موسیقی هر یک باب هشتم در بیان سازها و آلتها باب اول در بیان منشا و مبدا

علم موسیقی بر ارباب خبرت و اصحاب فطنت مخفی مباد

و محتجب نماند که در مبدا پیدایش این علم اختلافات بغایت

فرع الاستماع گردیده و باستماع در رسیده که بعضی بر آنند

که مهتر موسی صلوات الله تعالی علی نبینا و علیه وقتی که در وادی نیل

و در آن میان آب سنگی دید از جبرئیل علیه السلام پرسید که این

سنگ چیست مهتر جبرئیل گفت بر گیر که ترا بکار خواهد آمد

مهتر موسی علیه السلام آن سنگ را برداشت و با خود نگه میداشت

تا هنگامی که با قوم خویش بصحرای رسیده و جمله در آنجا

گذاشت و بر قدما آب آنخوالی خالی شدند و خلق از آتش

عطش بجان آمدند حضرت موسی علیه السّلام دست مناجات
بجناب مجیب الدعوات بر داشت فرمان حضرت رب
العزت در رسید که یا موسی عصا خود بران سنگ بزن
تا قدرت من مشاهده فرمائی و تماشای غریب معائنه نمائی
مهتر موسی عصا بران سنگ زد بقدرت سبحانه ازان
سنگ چشمهائی آب عذب جاری کردیدند و آب هر چشمه
بقومی رسید و از هر چشمه صدای اصول انتهای موسیقی
فی سحقی بر می آید بعد ازان یای موسی و حرف فی و حاء حقی
از وسط کلام بجهة کثرت استعمال محذوف کردانیده
و باقی موسیقی نامیدند و بعضی برانند که در شب معراج حضرت
رسالتمآب علیه و آله الصلوة و التسلیمات خلعت می خرد

در جهت وتین اسرار الهی بحر معرفت پوشیدند با ختیار اظهار

و ابهار بعض اسرار مامور گردیدند هر گاه که از عالم علوی بعالم

سفلی رسیدند پرده آن بعض اسرار پیش بادشاه

دلدل سوار و صاحب سیف ذو الفقار دریدند آن صیقل

شرک خفی و جلی یعنی حضرت مرتضی علی کرم الله وجهه طاقت

ضبط آن نیاورده بجناب رسالت مآب عرض شکایت

عدم محارست خود در میان آورده حضرت رسالت پناه

صلی الله تعالی علیه و آله و سلم فرمودند که زنهار زنهار ای اسد الله

دفینه این نغمه از گنجینه سینه بیرون نباید نهاد در صورت تعذر

از امکان مقدور بجایی صحرائی که نشان آبادی نداشته باشد

سر فرو آورده از هوا اندرون بیرون باید داد حضرت

در جهت ذیل اسرار الٰهی بحر معرفت پوشیدند باختیار اظهار

و اظهار بعض اسرار مامور گردیدند هرگاه که از عالم علوی بعالم

سفلی رسیدند پرده آن بعض اسرار پیش بادشاه

دلدل سوار و صاحب سیف ذو الفقار دریدند آن حقیقت

شرک خفی و جلی یعنی حضرت مرتضی علی کرم الله وجهه طاقت

ضبط آن نیاورد بجناب رسالت مآب عرض شکایت

عدم محارست خود درمیان آورد حضرت رسالت پناه

صلی الله تعالی علیه و آله وسلم فرمودند که زنهار زنهار یا اسد الله

دفینه این نعمه از گنجینه سینه بیرون منهاد نهاد در صورت تعذر

از امکان مفقود به چاهی صحرائی که نشان آبادی نداشته باشد

سر فرو آورده از هواء اندرون بیرون باید داد حضرت

مرتضی علی کرم الله وجهه از کثرت استیلا درونه رو به صحرا
آوردند و جای ویرانه فارغ از عمارات یافتند و اندران جایی
که در تنگی و تاریکی نظیر نداشت بدست آورده روی مبارک
دران فرا برده دامن جواهر اسرار نهانی از دست بسیطی قطرے
فرو هشت و آب مسکن جنبش فزون از چاه جوشش و خروش
کرده لب لبالب گشت و جانوران نواحی آن ویرانه
تحرک آب بر حسب مراد انگاشته روی توجه بدان آوردند
هنوز از نوشیدن آب سیر نگشته بودند که صیاد و صید جویی
بر سر آنها چنان تاخت که فی الحال نقد معاش آنها از دست
داده بدام کمند مقید ساخت و در حالت مستی نغمه ها
دلکش سرائیدن گرفتند و از شاخی بشاخی آویختند

حتی که درانحالت بجهری سر شاخها چون نوک سنان از

شکم آنها تجاوز نموده نور و نای آنها مانند ریسمان بسر هر

شاخ تنیده بعد از خشک گردیدن اصوات خوش یعنی نغمهای

دلکش از انها بر می آمدند و خاطر گیر هر شارع الطریق میگشت

وارباب عشق وشوق واصحاب محبت و ذوق از

مشاهده این حالت عجیب و از معاینه این حال غریب

حیران همی ماندند وچون این ترانه استماع اصول نشانه را

بر زبان میراندند بیت خشک تار و خشک چوب و خشک پوست

از کجا می آید این آواز دوست وازان آواز جا کند از قواعد

موسیقی بر بستند و بعضی اهل هند جریده موسیقی بر بن هستند

که در اصل توالد و تناسل اصول و فروع شجره این علم

و مزامیر با این همه اشکال بلوتون و ترکیب مزین از گوالیار است

که او را جامع هنر و منبع غنا میگویند و استادان تمام

این اشکال ازو میجویند و مکشوف باد که بجز نادهوان همین

هیچکس دم مساوات بگوالیار نزده است و ازو رساله

الیست اندرین فن بتسمیه پرم پارمان بعبارت که در

استحکام قوانین و قواعد نظیری ندارد و بعده بیکاس

درین هم مخلص آنست و او مردی بود که درین معامله ثانی

خود نداشت هرگاه صدای برمیکشید مرغ از پریدن در

هوا بایستادی و بار از رحم نسوان می افتاد و بعده بیجو باوره

که او را بیجو باوره نیز گویند و میر صاحب موصوف هم بدرجه

اتم رسیده واند بلکه میر صاحب را در سرائیدن راک دیپک

ستیاق ذکره بر چه بوده و ترجیح است چنانکه از روایان صاحب
تحقیق و محققان صاحب تدقیق محقق و مثبت کردند که
از سرائیدن این راگ بهیچ متنفس بهره و نرسیده و سماعش
بدون میرتانسین داو ستاوش از کسی قرع الاسماع نکرده
و آن مرغیست نر بماده و دراز منقار خانه زنبور وار سوراخ وار
که از هر رخنه اش نغمه پردازد و هر سوراخش ترنمی آغازد و
و هر دم خس و خاشاک فراهم می سازد تا وقتی که نای منقارش را
بنغمه دیپک می نوازد و از التهاب شعله آتشینش خس و خاشاک
بر افروزد و خود درمیان میسوزد و بعد از انقضاء زمانی خاکسترش
بقدرت او سبحانه بصورت بیضه می گراید و از آنجا بعد چند
بیست ایام از میانش مرغی محروق می برآید و نامش ولک

هنده و بنگ لات شهرت پذیر است و بپارسی آنرا آتش زبان
میگویند و بعد سپری نقش نقش و مکان طیرانش بیابانی است
وسیع که هیچکس در فسحت میدانش قدمی نزده و هیچ
کامی هست و محن صعوبت آتش نکشیده مگر میرزا حسین
که برای آموختن راگ مذکور دستیاری امداد فیض بنیاد
حضرت محمد غوث گوالیری قدس سره که میر موصوف
اولا بخدمت آنحضرت به تلبس خلعت تلقین کلمه طیب
مشرف گردیده و بعد مجاهده زمان سعد و وه باستمداد امداد
خرقه ولایت پوشیده و در آنجا رسیده و بعین حقیقین بعینه
حالات مسطوره آن مرغ دیده و گوشش هوش را به صدای
آتشش انجلای سرایدن نغمه دیگش برگماشت و آواز آنرا

محفوظ داشت و از انجا مراجعت نموده تا روزی میرتانسین

و نانک بیجو بانوره ماهر این فن بکمال نانک کوپال و نانک

اودهر بچهور و نانک صبرتخان و پلاس خان و چاند خان

و نانک رامداس و دیگر ماهران موسیقی که اندرین فن

مهارت تمام و تجارت تمام میداشتند بدرگاه فلک

بادشاه جهان پناه ظل الله حاضر بودند و باشارت فیض

بشارت شهنشاهی و امر جلیل القدر ظل اللهی سبحانه

موسیقی می نمودند حتی که هر یک از نانکان زبان انکار در حق

میرتانسین میکشودند و دعوی انا خیر منه می نمودند القصه چون

[illegible] بسرحد رسید اطناب خیام مباحثت بکرلیک

بین شرط کسسته گردید که اگر میر معز الیه بالتهاب شعله تاب

محفوظ داشت و از انجا مراجعت فرمود تا روزی میر تانسین
و نایک بیجو باوره ماهر این فن بکمال نایک گوپال و نایک
اودهر بچهو و نایک [illegible] تحان و پلاس خان و چاند خان
و نایک راداس و دیگر ماهران موسیقی که اندرین فن
مهارت تمام و مخارت تمام میداشتند بارگاه فلک
بادشاه جهان پناه ظل اله حاضر بودند و باشارت فیض
بشارت شهنشاهی و امر جلیل القدر ظل اللهی مباحثه
موسیقی می نمودند حتی که هر یک از نایکان زبان انکار در حق
میر تانسین میکشودند و دعوی اتاخیر مینمودند القصه چون
تم ولا متکلم بسرحد رسید اطناب خیام مباحثت بکرانه
بین شرط گسسته کردند که اگر میر معز الیه بالتهاب شعله تاب

او ای صدای راگ دیپک شمع و چراغ یک بیک

افروخته گردانید هر یک بجد مشق نیاز ارادت عمیری تقدیم

رسانند میر ناسین فی الفور از میان مجمع مباحثه برخاسته

دفتیلها و چراغها آب تر و پرساخته بر کنارهای حوض خاص

سرای شاهی نهادند و خود شمع بر کف دست افراشته

و میانش نزد فواره بایستاد و بسرائیدن آغاز آورد صدای

حرارت آثار راگ مذکور از الحان شعله افشان برکشیده

واز شعله افشانی آن ستر انداتش زبانه آب وشمع و چراغان

یک بیک روشن گردید و حرارت سوزش آتشش در دل

و کبد دماغش تا بجان رسید که بعد از مداومت و ملازمت

بتبرید مزید درنادی آوخته وافروده ازمنه شکارتر و غلامات شفقت

رو نما گردید پس هر یکی از مباحثان لبساط تجرد و نشاط بیار بگسترد
و هر واحدی از ناگهان سجدات شکرانه تمیزانه بجا آوردند
و والی مملکت خلعت فاخره در پوشانید و بنعمت وافر
و انعام متکاثر موفور السرور گردانید و تحقیق منشا اصول
بمبحث تعداد آنها اینجا خواهد یافت انشاء الله تعالی

باب دوم

در بیان انواع سماع بر وجدان ضمیر آئینه نظیر ارباب
تحقیق و اصحاب تدقیق لائح باد که سماع بر چهار نوع است
یکی حرام محض دویم مکروه سیوم مباح چهارم مستحب
پس حرام است برای آنکه او را از شنیدن سماع حب دنیا
زیاده شود و اخلاق ردیه بر خاطرش مستولی گردد و مباح است
مر آنکس را که حظ میکرد از صوت لطیف بتصور آنکه نه بر خاطرش

اوصاف رذائل طاری گردد و نه اخلاق محموده مستولی
و مکروه است مر آنکسی را که می‌شنود آنرا علی سبیل اللهو
بغیر تلذذ از آواز لطیف و سوای استبداد اخلاق حمیده
و طریان اوصاف و عادات ردیه و مندوب است
مر سالک طریقت را که باستماع عشق از بیدار و محو صوری
خلاصی یابد و بنهانخانه معنوی می‌شتابد کما قیل
فِی دستورِ القضاة قالَ الامامُ الغزالی رحمة
اللهِ تعالی علیهِ انَّ السَّماعَ قد یکونُ حراماً
محضاً و قد یکونُ مکروهاً و قد یکونُ
مباحاً و قد یکونُ مندوباً اَمَّا الحرامُ فهو لِاکثرِ
النَّاسِ مِنَ الشَّبابِ و مَن غلبَ علیهِ الشهوة

أي شهوة الدنيا فلا يحرك السماع منهم إلا ما
هو الغالب على قلوبهم من الصفات المذمومة
وأما المباح فهو لمن لا حظ له منه إلا التلذذ
بالصوت الحسن وأما المكروه فهو لمن لا
ينزله على صورة المخلوقين لكن يتخذه عادة له
في أكثر الأوقات على سبيل اللهو وأما المندوب
فهو لمن غلب عليه حب الله تعالى ومن لا يحرك
السماع منه إلا الصفات المحمودة و در مشايخ
چشتیه استماع سماع بمنزله فرض است و اگر انکار میکند
حلت سماع را على طريق الاجمال پس انکار کرده باشد مقام
صدیق را کما ذکر فی دستور القضاة قال

أي شهوة الدنيا فلا يحرك السماع منهم إلا ما

هو الغالب على قلوبهم من الصفات المذمومة

وأما المباح فهو لمن لا حظ له منه إلا التلذذ

بالصوت الحسن وأما المكروه فهو لمن لا

ينزله على صورة المخلوقين لكن يتخذه عادة له

في أكثر الأوقات على سبيل اللهو وأما المندوب

فهو لمن غلب عليه حب الله تعالى ومن لا يحرك

السماع منه إلا الصفات المحمودة ونزد مشايخ

چشتیه استماع سماع بمنزله فرض است و اکثر انکار میکنند

حلت سماع را علی طریق الاجمال پس انکار کرده باشند مقام

صدیق را کما ذکر في دستور القضاة قال

الشيخ ابو طالب المكي رحمة الله تعالى عليه

من انكر السماع مجملا اى مطلقا فقد انكر

سبعين صديقا، وذكر فيه ايضا وقال ذو النون

رحمة الله تعالى عليه السماع رسول حق جاء

يزعج القلوب الى الحق من اصغى اليه بحق تحقق

ومن اصغى اليه بنفس تزندق. وقيل ان الميل

وقع الى النداء من يوم الميثاق حين قال الحق

الست بربكم وكل واحد يسمع الى صوت طيب

ينزعج بذلك الشوق الى نداء آخر من الحق. وقيل

ان الحق وعد عباده ان يسلم عليهم بقوله

سلام قولا من رب رحيم فاذا وصل الى

الأذن صوت طيب تزعجت القلوب شوق إلى

سماع السلام الموعود . وقيل السماع للعارفين

غذاء الروح الفرض استماع سماع برای آنکس که نفس او

مرده و دل او زنده صحیح است و در حق غیر ایشان کس حکم

علی حسب ما ینبأ السماع . وعن عائشة رضی الله

تعالی عنها قالت إن أبا بكر دخل عليها

وعندها جاريتان في أيام منى تدففان وتضربان

وفيه وانهما تغنيان بما تقاولت الأنصار يوم

بعاث والنبي صلى الله عليه وسلم متغش

بثوبه فانتهرهما أبو بكر فكشف النبي صلى

الله عليه وسلم عن وجهه فقال دعهما يا أبا بكر

وفي رواية يا ابا بكر ان لكل قوم عيدا وهذا

عيدنا متفق عليه وهذا الحديث تدارك في

المشكات واما مزامير پس حكمش درفتاوي شامي بطريق

واضح مذكور است وعبارتش بعينه اين است وذكر

في رسالة امام العلامة مجتهد العصر فخر الدين

الرازي رحمة الله تعالى عليه المزامير يوجدها في

الاصوات الموزون وهو بالنظر الى نفسه

مباح كما ذكر واما الحرمة فبعلة الاخرى وهو

التذكر عند شرب الخمر كما روى الثقات

عن النبي صلى الله عليه وسلم اذا حرم الخمر

حرم المزامير اذا الناس يطربون وقت شربه

نحرم ضربه لتذكيره وهو قبيح لمعنى في غيره

فإذا كان هذه العلة مفقودة تفقد حرمته

ايضا فلهذا يباح ضرب الطبل في الحروب والعرس

وضرب الطبل في الأوقات الخمس وفي غير

الأوقات حرام فثبت أن الحكم متغير

بتغير العلة وإذا كانت النفس ذاهبة عن اللهو

والهواء وموصوفة بالصفوة والذكاء وتستأنس

بمشاهدته تعالى واللقاء فأصوات المزامير

داعية من الكدر إلى الصفاء ومزلفة من

السفل إلى العلاء والصوت صفوة الحسن وهي

قوة الأرواح وقوتها في عالم الملكوت انتهى

و لهذا قیل اسماء رسول الحق والله تعالی اعلم

باب سیوم در بیان اوازات موافق انکه استادان و

ماهران این فن تا سیز تمیز را باستلزام کرده هفت

سُر و شادول استراند بر تراند با انها قبیل ائمه در ع سمره و تعلیم

فرموده اند واز ایجاد خصائل نراکی عشره در دیه تاکید اکید شده

نموده اند واین هفت سُر را مقدمه استراند گفته اند و استراند

را مقدمه تراند پس معنی با لازم که باستلزام علم وماتت واعمال

ممنوعات ساعی بجان باشد فاما علم وماتت سبعه پس نام یکی

از انها کهرج است ونام دوم رکب ونام سیوم کندهار

ونام چهارم مدهم ونام پنجم پنچم ونام ششم دهوت

ونام هفتم نکهاد وبرای زکاوت انجلای احبار ارکیا و

محتجب نماند که این ملزومات اصولی است که ناشی گردیده اند

از الحان طیب البیان طیور مگر صوت سایع که منشاء اش

آواز ابابیت بید است و آنرا بفارسی بیل سفید گویند

و درعربی فیل محسو و و اسامی نامی اطیار شیرین مقال

اینست کهرج و این مرغیست مشهور که آنرا بپارسی طاوس

نامیده اند و جاترک چنانک کهرج و کوکلا و ترنک فیستا

الصَّوتُ الاَوَّلُ صَوتُ الاَوَّلِ مِن هٰذِهِ الطُّیور

وَالثّانی مِنهَا فَقِس عَلٰی هٰذَا مَا بَقِیَ وَاما

ممنوعات عشره پس یکی از انها ترقی ال است کما

سَیَجِیئُ ذِکرُهُ فِی البابِ الثّامِنِ و دوم نغمه بیان

سیوم مشابهت صوت مغنی بصوت کلاغ چهارم سرود

پی سروبی استراد یعنی پی آلاب پنجم زدن چاین به چین
ششم هنگام سرود کردن جنبانیدن هفتم روی
بلتقین کردانیدن هشتم اندراج یعنی آمیزش یک سر
بدیگر سر نمودن نهم صدای ترانه و استراد از راه بینی
و دماغ برآوردن دهم اعضا جنبانیدن باب چهارم

در بیان تعداد اصول و فروع و اشاره برآرائی دیانت پیرائی ارباب
ذوی الباب مخفی و محتجب نماند که باصطلاح موسیقین اساس
قواعد علم موسیقی اصول موصوفه کنایت از راگها سی
ستة است و فروع کنایة از راگنیهای ثلثین واما
انقار پس من بعد لحاظ تعبیر اصول بازدواج و تعبیر فروع بزوجات
آنها کنایت است از راگها که بعد تناسب اجنبیت آنها

بازواج مذکوره ملقب و معبر نموده اند انهارا بپسران اصول

یعنی پسران راگهای سته و کنایت از راگها و راگنیهاست

که نسبت شاسن انهارا بپسرون و زوجات نموده اند

وَهِيَ كَمَا لَا تُعَدُّ وَلَا تُحْصَى وَسَيَأْتِي اسْمُ

كُلِّ وَاحِدٍ مَعْلُومٌ بِمَشِيَّتِهِ سُبْحَانَهُ پس راگ اول

از راگهای سته نام آن بهیروست و نام دوم مالکوس

و نام سیوم هندول و نام چهارم دیپک و نام پنجم

سری راگ و نام ششم میگهه و منشا راگ بهیرو از صدای

الحان روح داودی علیه السلام که هنگام استماع آوردن

روح آدم علیه السلام از قدوم و رستگاری جسم از جنات

تقدس تاب او سبحانه مامور گردیده و استراز فرحت شاه

سرور انگیز نغمه و آمیز برکشیده و روحش از جام شراب
لذتش بیهوش گردیده بجنبید و آرامید چنانچه مشهور
و متعارفست و راگ مالکوس از صدای سرور آثار
آواز ترانه ساز الحان لذت افزای لطافت توامان
نزاکت التیام مهتر جبرئیل علیه السلام پیدا گردید و مبدأ
راگ هندول از استرانه ترانه الحان طیب البیان رضوان
باغبان جنان هویدا گردید و مبداء راگ دیپک از صداء
شور افزای هنگام طلوع هور است و منشاء سری راگ
آواز جانگداز اژدهائیست که تحت الثری تمام دوره
زمین را با حافظه طولانی خود گذاشته و باره دم خود
بنا بر کشیدن سمومش دهان فرا داشته و منشاء راگ

میکهیه اختلافست نزد بعضی از محققان آواز رعد است

ونزد بعضی از مدققان از صدا، گردش دور دوار

چرخ تیز رفتار است و پوشیده مباد و محجوب نماناد

که علامت انتهار اعتدال صدا بهیر و آنست که رجی بدون

کشش شور خود بخود دیگر و دو صورتی حاضر شود که جامهای

سفید پوشیده و سوار کاو بر پوست آهو نشسته بسبحه

سرهای آدمی در گلو آویخته و کنگن زر در بند دست انداخته

سیمایش همچو بدر تابان باشد و علامت انتهای استوا

صدا، عالکوس آنست که با عضاء سامع چنان حرارتی

وشوری پیدا گردد که زبان حالش برین بیت مترنم شود فرد

چست رقصانم که اندر آتشم ... پای کوبانم که اندر آتشم

وصورت مرد و اندر سیما گندم گون جامها سیاه معطر

پوشیده و سبحه دانه گوهر با بکلو آویخته و در حلقه زنان عنبرین

موی سمن بوی کمان ابرو لطیف الجسم بر تخت نشسته باشد

هویدا و پیدا گردد و علامت اعتدال با کمال سرهند و آن است

که مهد خود بخود در جنبش آید بحدی که بسکون نگراید و شکل مرد

شایسته و خوبرو و گندم گون که بدر سیمایش مانند مهر سپهر تابان

و درخشان و افسر پادشاهی و تاج ظل اللهی بر سر و ملبوس زعفرانی

و بر بر بو متکلم شیرین منش فریبنده عالم باشد منبصر گردد و علامت

نهایت و غایت استوا صدا و کمال اعتدال استرانه ترانه

دیپک آنست که از آتش سامانی و شعله افشانی آن شمع

افروخته ماننده پروانه سوخته گردد و هیئت مرد قوی هیکل

چون مرد از لباس سرخ در بر پوشیده و تسبیح مرجان بچنگ آویخته

که از التهاب کلامش مشتعل از وحشت باشد حاضر گردد و علامت

غایت اعتدال نغمهٔ سری راگ آنست که از طراوت آتشش

درخت خشک سبز گردد و صورتی ملکانه سر برهنه گیسو دراز

بدست گل نیلوفر داشته و رشته شگفته پر از دو انهار بلور

گردن که نور از کلامش درخشان و تابان باشد بنمایش آید

و علامت انتهای صدا راگ میگهه آنست که ابر و بارش آید

و هیئت مرد شاد و دلاور و جهد ور مانند شیر غران و چهره اش

همچو هیبت سلاطین هنگام کین پر سیاست

و کسوت زرد و رنگ در بر پوشیده و زنان خوب صورت را

بزور خود کشیده و افسر بر سر و گلها بدست معاینه گردد

پیل سوار لباس سرخ در بر پوشیده و تسبیح مرجان بگلو آویخته

که از التهاب کلامش مشتعل افروخته باشد حاضر گردد و علامت

غایت اعتدال نغمه سری راگ آنست که از طراوت آبش

درخت خشک سبز گردد و صورت ملکانه سر برهنه گیسو دراز

بدست گل نیلوفر داشته و رشته شگفته پر از و انها بلور

کرده که نور از کلامش درخشان و تابان باشد بنمایش آید

و علامت انتهای صدای میگهه آنست که ابر در بارش آید

و هیئت مرد بشاور و دلاور چهره مانند شیر غران و چهره اش

همچو هیبت سلاطین هنگام کین پر سیاست

و کسوت زر در رنگ در بر پوشیده و زنان خوب صورت را

بنزد خود کشیده و افسر بر سر و کلاها بدست معاینه گردد

والله اعلم بالصواب و هویدا باد که مر هر یک راگ را
ازین راگهای سته پنج راگنیها مقرر است پس آن پنج
راگنیها که برای راگ بهیرو معین شده اند نام یکی از انها
بهیرمیت ونام دوم آبهیری ونام سیوم مدومادهوی
ونام چهارم سیندوی ونام پنجم بنگالی و آن پنج راگنیها
معینهٔ مالکوس اسم یکی از انها تودی است و اسم دوم
دهناسری و اسم سیوم دهول سری و اسم چهارم
کن کلی و اسم پنجم کنبهاوتی و آن راگنیهای خمسه که
برای راگ هندول معین اند نام یکی از انها رامکلی است ونام
دوم دیوساکهه ونام سیوم للت بفتح اللام الاول والثانی
مع التشدید ونام رالت کته بخلاف الثالث بفتح اللام الاول

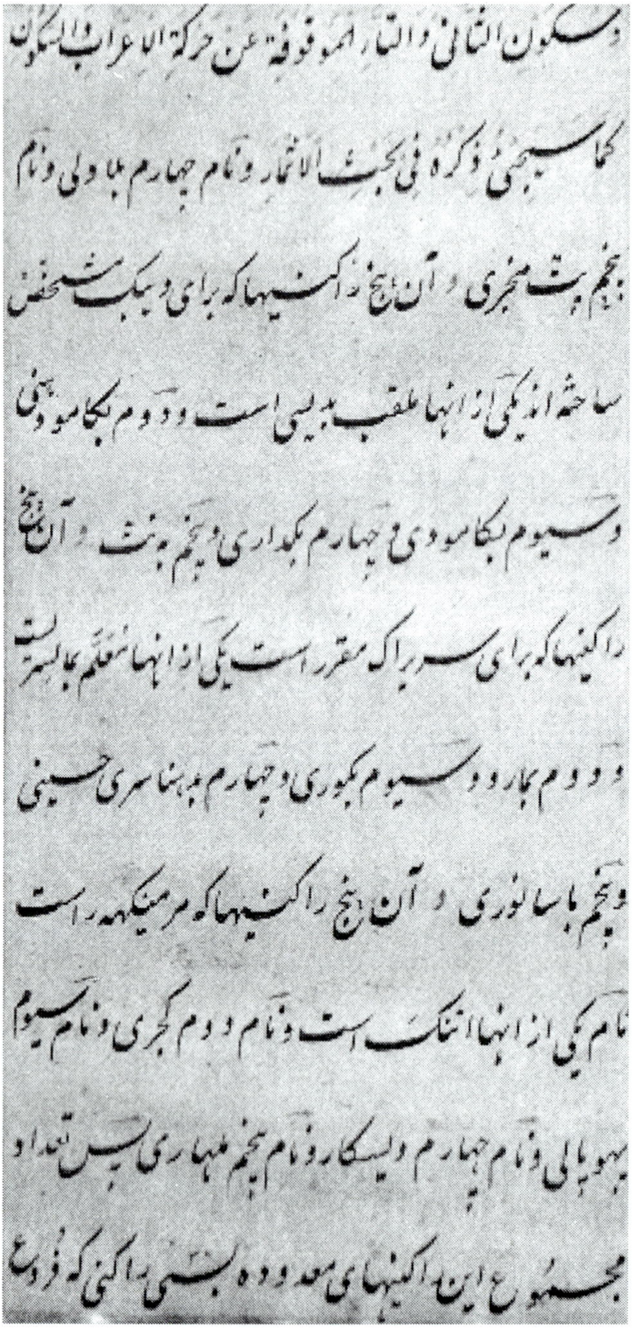

وسکون الثانی والثالث الموقوفة عن حرکة الاعراب السکون

کما سیجیٔ ذکره فی بحث الاثمار و نام چهارم بیلاولی و نام

پنجم پت منجری و آن پنج راگنیها که برای دیپک مشخص

ساخته اند یکی از انها ملقب بدیسی است و دوم بکاسودهی

و سیوم بکاسودهی چهارم بکداری پنجم پنث و آن پنج

راگنیها که برای سری راگ مقرر است یکی از انها معلم مالسری است

دوم مارو و سیوم گوری چهارم دهناسری حسینی

پنجم باسالوری و آن پنج راگنیها که مر میگهه راست

نام یکی از انها تنک است و نام دوم گجری و نام سیوم

بهوپالی و نام چهارم دلیسکار و نام پنجم ملهاری پس تعداد

مجموع این راگنیهای معدوده بسی راگنی که فروع

کنایت از انها نمود و اند خواهد پرداخت و تعیین اسامی اینها

اختلافات بینهایات منصور گردیده اما تحقیق تعیین به اینها

در رسید و تعیین اسامی از ماهران موسیقی استادان این فن

شنیده و آن راگها که نسبت بنوت و ابنیت آنها

به راگها رسته نموده اند و اینها را پسران آنها مقرر فرموده اند

به چهل و شش تن چنانچه برای هر راگ هشت پسر معین ساخته اند

اما آن هشت پسر که برای راگ بهیرو مقرر کرده اند نام

یکی از انها کرنجم ست و نام دوم بهرش و نام سیوم و ساو

و نام چهارم بنگال و نام پنجم مده و نام ششم مادهو بفتح الدال

و سکون الهاء و نام هفتم کرناوی و نام هشتم مشکلابلاول

و آن هشت پسر که برای راگ مالکوس مشخص نموده اند

یکی از انها ویراک ماروا است و دوم میود و بسکون الدال

و سیوم بهینی منشرنک و چهارم بروا و پنجم چندرکاسیس

و ششم سورتهه بضم السین و الواو الساکنة المجهولة والرآء

المهموقة من الحرکة والسکون وفتح التاء الهندیة والهاء

الساکنة و هفتم راج بهر او هشتم نندا و اما هشت پسر راگ

هندول پس نام یکی از انها منکل آشتک است و نام دوم

تیکا چندر و نام سیوم چنچل و نام چهارم بهول نند و نام پنجم

بهیسا کهر و نام ششم ور دوس و نام هفتم بوتا و نام هشتم

بسنتا و آن هشت پسر که مرو بیکب را مقرر است نام

یکی از انجا بهنور کلیا نست و نام دوم دونل و نام سیوم رام

و نام چهارم کنولا و نام پنجم کرم بفتح الکاف العربیة والراء

و نام ششم تنجاب و نام هفتم کاموده نا و نام هشتم هما لاو

آن هشت پسر که برای سُر براک معین نموده اند یکی از انها

مالی گوره است و دوم سارنگا و سیوم سوربنک و چهارم

دیوکنده ناره و پنجم سهرای نتک و ششم بادرکونده بداول هندی

که ور آخر است و هفتم تنک بهاگوک و هشتم آتهیرا و آن هشت

پسر که برای سین کهه مقرر ساخته اند نام یکی از انها کانرا است

و نام دوم دهنشر و نام سیوم کدارا و نام چهارم جلندهر

و نام پنجم گجدهر و نام ششم سوهب و نام هفتم بک هربوتا

بالبار و الدال الهندیه شین و نام هشتم سنکرابرن و دراسم

پسران هم اختلاف بی نهایت است اما قول اصح همین است

که مذکور گردید و صحت تعلم آنها بتصحیح رساله گوالیار و اما آن

راگها و راگنیها که نسبت تناسل آنها بشوند و زوجات

موصوفه و زوجات بنون که جمله آنها مشتمل از ازواج چهل و شش

معین ساخته اند چنانچه از برای هر یک پسر یک زوجه مقرر است

و از جهة کثرت اختلاف در اسامی و تعیین آنها و عدم دریافت

اقوال صحیحه متمسک بهر یک بعدا و آنها نگاه رفته و در اسامی

آنها در رشته نسیانی و تکاسل سفته و در رسیده و لی

شمار آنها از وسعت اندازه عدد و فسحت اسامی آنها از احاطه

حد بیرون منصور گردیده که اگر تمامه ذکر نموده آید البته دفتری

دیگر می باید لیکن آنقدر که شهرت پذیر گردیده اند بقید قلم

در رسیده اند و مجموع آنها یکصد و پنجاه و دو خواهد بود

چنانچه چاولا و چاول و بسنت و بسنتی و للت و للتی

بفتح اللام الاول و سکون الثانی بخلاف للت بفتح الاول

و الثانی مع التشدید و آن راگنی سیوم راگ هندول است

کامود و سارنگ و ملهار و پوریا و پوربی و سهری و بعضی منسوب

که سری راگ و سری کی راگ است و بهیم و پوریا و پلاس

ترمن و جنی و مارو و گورا و سیام و کامود و کلیان و

بهاگ و کنماج و بهج و ججونتی و سورتهه بخلاف سورتهه

بفتح الثانی التشدید و کبهار و بهیار و بهبهاس و لیلکا

و اسا و صندوری و گوند و ایمن و ایمنی و غاره و جوگاوتی

و آسکندی و کداری و بهار و کنوس و بعضی با کلوش و

کونس را گراک شمرده اند و پرچیا و کدارا و ترون و

دیب و لی و لاچاری و سکهری و حسینی و بیلو

و بهیرسی و اوانا و ش بهانا و سنکهراوی و بنکلی و دیسری

و مالجهنک و بهاوی و برهنس و پرجهرا و جیت و سارنک

و سارنکی و دیسکی و منکلی و هنپر و هنپری و دیک اندهار

و این را دیوکندهار که پسر چهارم سری راک است نیز میکویند

و نیز و بعضی متغایر اند و کلب راک و کورا و ساکهید و کالیک

و هندولی و کنونسیه و ناکرو بهاکی و سوتا و بلاس و آسی

و دهول و پردوی سورتهه و کرلا و تی و کهت و غاریق و کجری

و پردیپکی و دیک هاری و سونکی و پردی و تلنک و بهیم

و چلکاری و سورتی و کهنبهاوی و سنکری و بهاکی و جک

پرجیا و نیلو و ناد و بهیمی و جهری و کندهاری و اشلکند و

کنباجی و بهاوتی و کوندکی و رامی و بهاری و لاتکهوتی و سورجی

واکن جوتی و سنفرستی و پکلون الفار و پلاسری و گورکلی

و جیتی و للنک سن و کورن و مالوا و کندهار و براری و نونات

و بہتی و دیسکلا و جوراشنک و ساونک ناک سوہا

و راج بنس و کلابل و جیتر بہولا و و بسن کلی و ترون و

للهاوتی و تنک و بہولا راک و سروتک شام و کہنی و

سنک کرمن و کبسیری و بہیروی و بہاگی و جکیب

و برای و کورکلی و سندری و کنندکی و کندهاری و کولا

و کھرم و سلیخا و لوبہہ و جیجونی و کلہانی و بنسی و دہرلے

و آستاوان و ماهران این فن انفراج و انشراح

این اسامی بنابر او خال بہما در آمیزہا و طونیها و برای تمہید

تقسیم متعارف بعضی از آنها کما سیاتی بزبان خامه می آید

ولهذا این اسامی را تمهید التقسیم و توطئة الترکیب میشمارند

باب پنجم دربیان تقسیم بعض اصول و فروع و اشعار

بدان ایدک الله تعالی فی حفظ الاقسام وعرفک

الله تعالی فی الانام که درینجا مراد از بعض اصول که کنایه

از راگهای ستة است کما مر فی بحث التعداد یعنی

راگ است و مراد از بعض فروع که کنایت از راگنیها

ثلثین است کما ذکر فی بابه ایضاً هفت راگنیهاست و پنج راگ

و بیست و سه راگنیهای دیگر قسمت نیز کرده اند کما

ذکره دلیل عدم الانقسام فی رسالة الطویلة

کبیه مر بادشاهان بهنادت و رسالة گوالیار

و غیرها اما آن یک راگ که منقسم میشود بهیرو است و اقسامش

بچهار رسیده یکی بهیرو شده و دوم کنبری و سیوم کرل

و چهارم سکیا سنکهیرن و برای هر یکی ازین چهار قسم

یک غنچه یعنی کلی مقرر است و اینجا کلی عبارت از دختر است

پس هر یکی را از چهار اقسام بهیرو و یک غنچه یعنی یک دخترک

خواهد بود پس غنچه بهیرو سده کن کلی است و غنچه کنبری را

مکلی و غنچه کرل سنکهیرن کلی و غنچه سکیا سنکهیرن پرکاس

کلی و اما آن هفت راگنیها که منقسم میشوند پس یکی ازانها

توری است که اول راگنی مالکونس است کما علمت و آنرا

توڑی نیز میگویند اما صحیح توری است و دوم بنت منجری که

راگنی پنجم هندول است و سیوم نت که پنجم راگنی دیپک است

و چهارم مالسری که اول راگنی سریراک است و پنجم کوری ک

راگنی تهانی راگ مذکور است و ششم اسانوری که راگنی

پنجم این راگ است هفتم گجری که راگنی دوم راگ

میگهه است پس توری منقسم میشود بده قسم یکی توری

سده و دوم توری هیراری و سیوم توری بهادری

چهارم توری دیسی و پنجم توری جونپوری و ششم توری

اسانوری و هفتم توری منگلیکهه و هشتم توری لاچاری

و نهم توری یوناکی و دهم توری کهت سوائی کهت تانسینی

که اظهر من الشمس است و بدین قسم مغایرت تمام و مباینت

تام میدارد و بعد این هر دو راگنی می انگارد و بهت منجری دو

قسم است یکی تانسینی دوم سورداسی و نت منقسم میشود

بهفت قسم یکی نت سده و دوم نت کدار و سیوم نت

ملهار چهارم نٹ نراین پنجم نٹ آهیری و ششم نٹ
نارو و هفتم نٹ سانورین و مالسری چهار قسم است یکی
سری سده دوم جیت سری سیوم پرتاب سری چهارم
دهول سری و کوری منقسم میکردد به دو قسم یکی کوری سده
دوم کوری جیتی و بعضی بعکس الترتیب نیز میکویند
یعنی جیتی کوری اما فی الاصل لفظ کوری مقدمست بر جیتی
کما فی القسم الاول و اسانوری سه قسم است یکی اسانوری
سده دوم اسانوری جوکیا سیوم اسانوری صورتخان
و کجری هم منقسم میکردد به سه قسم یکی ازانها کجری سده است
دوم کهت کجری و سیوم سیام کجری و هویدا باد که در نخ
مرا و از بعض اثمار شجره موصوفه که آنها کنایت از بنون

اصول و از شش اصل منسوب به بیستون زوجات بودند نوزده اند

یکی از آنها بلاول است و دویم للت بفتح الاول و سکون

الثانی و سیوم ساکهه و چهارم سارنگ پنجم ملهار و ششم

پوربا و هفتم گورا و هشتم جوک و نهم سیام و دهم کامود

و یازدهم کلیان و دوازدهم کانرا و سیزدهم بهاک

و چهاردهم کدارا و پانزدهم سنکهرا و شانزدهم کهنباج

و هفدهم بیج و هژدهم جیجوتی و نوزدهم سورتهه بس بلاول

منقسم میشود بچهارده قسم یکی از آنها بلاول شده

دویم بلاول گلب و سیوم بلاول سکل و چهارم بلاول

الهیا و پنجم بلاول کهنباجی و ششم بلاول جیجوتی و هفتم

بلاول سنکرا و هشتم بلاول کچهیلی و بعضی بالعکس الترتیب

گویند بهیلی بلاول و نهم بلاول امین و دهم کامودی بلاول

و یازدهم مدهر سیا بلاول و دوازدهم سکهیا بلاول و سیزدهم

بلاول سهاک و چهاردهم بلاول سیوتا و للت منقسم میشود

بچهار قسم یکی خود للت من غیر اتصاله بشیء آخر و دوم للتا

کدار و سیوم للت مار و چهارم للالتی و سا کهه که آنرا

من جهة النظر الی انه مدسا کهان میگویند نیز منقسم میشود

بچهار قسم یکی ازان دیو ساکهه است و دوم کن ساکهه

و سیوم لچهه ساکهه و چهارم بهسور ساکهه و سارنگ

منقسم میشود بیازده قسم یکی ازان سارنگ و ات

و دوم بندرابنی سارنگ و سیوم سارنگ پهنس و چهارم

طرهون سارنگ و پنجم ساونت سارنگ و ششم

دهوریا سارنگ و هفتم سورتهیه سارنگ و هشتم سهجا رنگ
سارنگ نهم سارنگ بدوانت و دهم گوبرماری سارنگ
یازدهم نهاری سارنگ و ملهار نیز منقسم میشود به یازده قسم
یکی از انها ملهار سده است دوم گوند ملهار و سیوم ملهار
دهوریا و چهارم مرهون ملهار و پنجم رامداسی ملهار و ششم
سورداسی ملهار و هفتم ساونت ملهار و هشتم سالونرین کی
ملهار و نهم میگهاولی ملهار و دهم بسنتی ملهار و یازدهم
هندولی ملهار و پوریا منقسم میشود به چهار قسم یکی پوریا سده
دوم پوریا دهناسری و سیوم پوریا بهیهاس و چهارم
پوریا کلیان و گورا نیز منقسم میشود به چهار قسم یکی از انها
گورا سده است دوم مالی گورا سیوم چیتی گورا چهارم

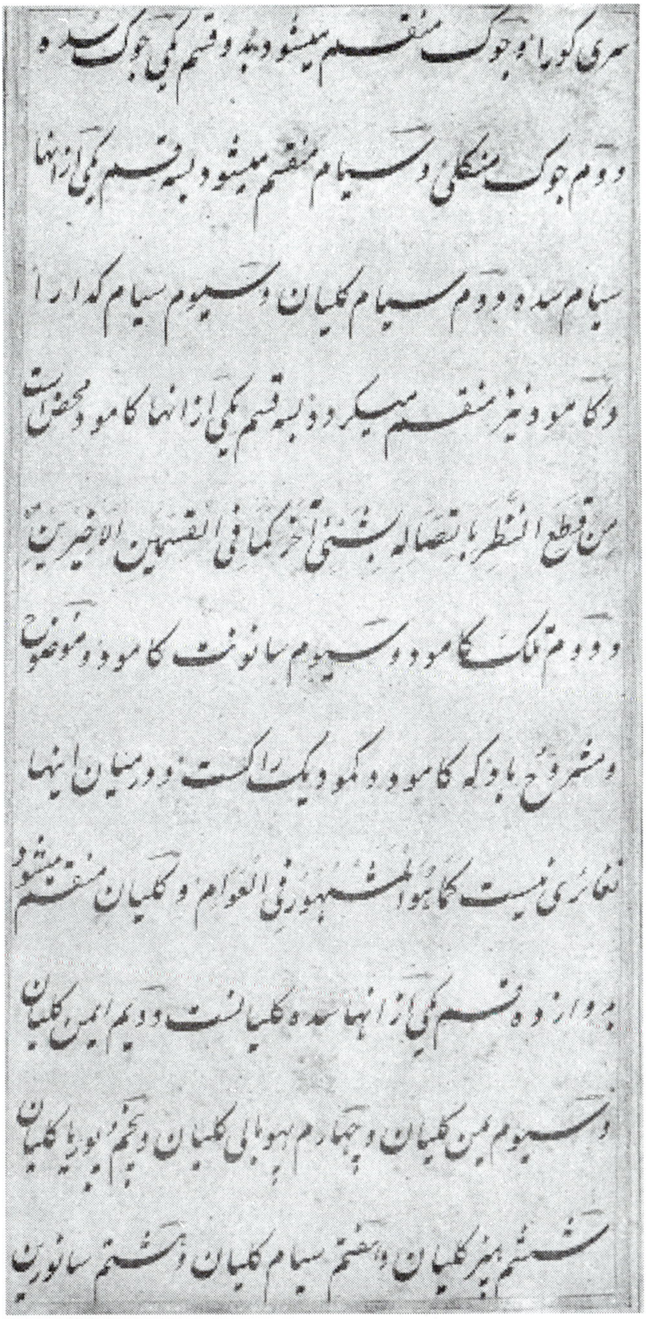

سری گوریا و جوگ منقسم میشود بدو قسم یکی جوگ سده و
دوم جوگ منگلی و سیام منقسم میشود به سه قسم یکی از آنها
سیام سده و دوم سیام کلیان و سیوم سیام کدارا
و کاموده نیز منقسم میگردد بسه قسم یکی از آنها کاموده محض است
من قطع النظر باتصاله بشئی آخر کما فی القسمین الاخیرین
و دوم تلک کاموده و سیوم سانونت کاموده و منوهر
و مشرح باوکه کاموده کمودیک را گفت و در میان اینها
تغایری نیست کما هو المشهور فی العوام و کلیان منقسم میشود
بر دوازده قسم یکی از آنها سده کلیان است دوم ایمن کلیان
و سیوم یمن کلیان و چهارم بهوپالی کلیان و پنجم پوریا کلیان
ششم هیر کلیان و هفتم سیام کلیان و هشتم سانورین

کلیان و نهم کامود کلیان دهم نت کلیان و یازدهم بهیم

کلیان و دوازدهم کهیم کلیان و کانرا منقسم میشود

بهشت قسم یکی از انها سده کانرا است دوم نایکی کانرا و سوم

سهانا کانرا و چهارم اڈانا کانرا و پنجم سکهری کانرا و ششم

اکیں کانرا و هفتم مندرکیهه کانرا و هشتم بکهیسری کانرا و نهم

کنوسیه کانرا و دهم بسنتی کانرا یازدهم کهنباجی کانرا و دوازدهم

سورتهیه کانرا سیزدهم جونتی کانرا چهاردهم درباری کانرا

پانزدهم کرناتی کانرا شانزدهم نارا کانرا هفدهم منکلک کهه

کانرا هژدهم دولتی کانرا و بهاک منقسم میشود بدو قسم

یکی بهاک سده دوم بهاکرا و کدارا منقسم میگردد به پنج قسم

یکی از انها کدارا سده است و دوم سیام کدارا و سوم

نت کدارا و چهارم للتا کدارا و پنجم مار و کدارا و سنکرا

منقسم میشود بچهار قسم یکی ازانها سنکرا بهده است دوم سنکرا

برن و سیوم سنکرا اسنکهبرن و چهارم سنکرا ارن و کنهج

منقسم میشود بدو قسم یکی کنهاج بهده دوم پرچها کهماج

و پنج هم دو قسم میگردد یکی خود پنج بلا اتصال بشیی آخر

و دوم جوکیا پنج و چجونتی نیز منقسم میشود بدو قسم یکی

چجونتی بهده دوم چجونتی کانرا که سیزدهم کانرا مذکور گردید

و سوره تهه هم دو قسم است یکی سوره تهه بهده دوم سوره تهه

اسا نکت باب ششم در بیان درستی و همه این اصول

و فروع و بعضی اثار مذکوره بر ضمایر مهر نظایر ارباب فنی لهاب

نبرت شعار فیلت اثر و اصحاب ویانت اکتساب فرو

الا فی کار بعضی اطوار اختلاف رفته باشد که معلمان موسیقی

و ماهران این فن بتاکیدات بلیغات تا تمیز بر تمیز را

نگهداشت و یاد داشت اوقات و ساعات سرائیدن

راگها و راگنیها تعلیم فرموده اند و تشریح اوقات

ترنم و تصریح ساعات تغنم بدینسان نموده اند که هنگام

سرائیدن راگ بهیرو هفت گهری و چهار پل شبگیر یعنی آخر

شب مقرر است و احیان نغمه مالکونس از نیم شب

تا ابتداء وقت بهیرویست و نزد بعضی از نصف اللیل

تا طلوع الشمس و وقت آغاز نغمه راگ هندول آنست

که چون قدر سه گهری و شش پل مهر بر سپهر برآمده باشد و

سرائیدن شری آنست که چون فرصت یک گهری از یک

روز تجاوز نماید و نزد بعضی تمام یک پاس است یعنی از طلوع
آفتاب تا یکپاس روز و هنگام ترانه اشترانه و نیمکت از یکپاس
روز تا نیمروز و بعضی میگویند که هنگام سرائیدنش نیمشب است
اما قول اول بصحت در رسیده و وقت سرائیدن
سریراگ آنست که چون یکپاس از روز باقی مانده باشد
تا هنگام غروب روز و بعضی شش گهری و سه پل باقی
آخر روز است و هنگام سرائیدن میگهه وقت بارش
باران است و از نیمروز تا وقت زوال و بعد از گذشتن یکپاس
شب تا هنگامی که قدر دو گهری از نیمشب باقی مانده باشد اما
وقت بارش باران افضل الاوقات است و پوشیده نماند
که چنانکه استادان اهل فارس دوازده مقام را بمقابله

دوازده برج مقرر ساخته‌اند و فوز سرور الشان و ترانه هر یک

مقام در هنگام مراجعت مهر در برج مقامش شناخته‌اند

همچنان ماهران اصل هند هر یکی را از اصول سته بازاشهر بن

از مشهور جلال متعین نموده‌اند و بنا بر حصول لذت تمام

و حظ تام مغنیه هر یک راگ بشهرین محاویش امر فرموده‌اند

پس هر مغنی را بگفتار این سراپا انکسار گوش هوش باید

بر گماشت و معانی ذوات اسامی مشهور هر یک راگ محفوظ

باید داشت چنانچه شهریور و مهر ماه را برای راگ بهیرو متعین

ساخته‌اند و دی و بهمن را برای مالکونس و اسفندارمذ که آنرا

بالاختصار اسفندارمز گویند و فروردی را برای هندول و اردی

بهشت و خورداد را برای دیپک و آبان و آذر برای

سر براگ وتهر و مرواور ابرای میگهه وازانجا که حفظ

النظم اسهل من حفظ النثر واقعست لهذا این

دو بیت متضمن و محیط ماههای جلالی بتحریر و تسطیر یافت

ز فروردی چو بگذشتی مه اردی بهشت آمد ** بهمه خورداد

تیر آنکه چو مرداد وشت همی شاید ** پس از شهریور و مهر

ابان آذر و دی وان ** که بر بهمن جز اسفندارمذ ماهی نیفزاید

پس مستحسن آن مینماید که هر مترنم را شاید که نغمه بی هنگام

نسراید تا حرف تفاضل ابتدا ورا از لوحه طبیعت انسان نیه

بکلک تا هنگامی نزداید ا هنگام سرائیدن بهیرمی که راگنی

اول راگ بهیرو است از طلوع آفتاب است تا نیم پاس

روز و وقت نغمه ابهیری و مده مادهوی و سیندوی

و بنگالی بعد از منقضی گردیدن مقدار شش گهری روز است

تا یکپاس و اما وقت نغمه پردازی و ترانه سازی گوری

و دهناسری پس هنگامی است که قدر یکپاس و دو گهری کم

عصر بر سپهر بر آمده باشد لیکن این وقت آغاز نغمه ولیست

و هنگام انتهای ترانه اش گذشتن یک و نیم پاس و سه

گهری و سه پل مقرر نموده اند و هنگام سرائیدن دهنواسری

وقت نغمه کشیدن سریراگ است ابتدا و انتها کرسه پل کم

بشش گهری اتصال میدارند و رینجا لالیعنی و هنگام نغمه کنکلی

از پاس اخیر شب تا وقتیکه قدر نیم پاس از روز گذشته باشد

و تعیین هنگام ترانه کنهاتی عین نیم شب است و اما راگ کلی

وقت گنگلی دارد و هنگام نغمه دیوساکهه وقتی که قدر یکپاس

روز منقضی گردیده باشند و نیز بعضی قدرش یک پهر

تا یک و نیم پاس و هنگام آغاز ترانهٔ للت آنست که

چون قدر نیم پاس و یک گهری مهر بر سپهر بر آمده باشد

و انتهایش آنست که چون قدر یکپاس و دو گهری از روز

بگذرد و نیز وقت سرائیدنش از ظهر تا غروب مقرر است

و آغاز هنگام نغمهٔ بلاولی و هیر می یکیست و انتهایش

آنست که چون مقدار پنج گهری مهر بر سپهر علو نموده باشد

و اما وقت ترانهٔ بهت منجری از نیمروز تا غروب آفتابست

و اما ابتدا وقت سرائیدن ولیی پس انتهای هنگام ترانهٔ

بلاولیست و انتهایش نهایت هنگام نغمهٔ دیوساکه

و وقت ترانهٔ کامودهی بعد از گذشتن یکپاس شب است

تا نیم شب و هنگام نغمه کامودهنی و گداری از غروب

آفتاب است تا گذشتن مقدار دو گهری شب و ابتدا

هنگام سرا شدن نت قبیل از غروب شمس است

وانتهایش نهایت هنگام نغمه کامود است و اما

وقت شروع ترانه مالسری آنست که مقدار سه پاس

و دو گهری از روز منقضی گردیده باشد و انتهای هنگام سرا شدن

انکه چون مقدار دو گهری از روز باقی ماند و آغاز هنگام سرا شدن

مار و وقت ترانه کنهاوتی است و انتهایش انکه چون

قدر سه پاس و دو گهری از شب بگذرد و وقت نغمه

گوری بعد از گذشتن سه و نیم پاس و یک گهری روز

تا هنگام غروب آفتاب است و هنگام نغمه و هنا سری

حسینی بعد از انقضاء یکپاس روز است تا مقدار

گذشتن دو گهری و هنگام آغاز ترانه اساوری آنست

که مقدار شش گهری روز مهر بر سپهر برآمده باشد و وقت

انتهای ترانه اسش هنگام انتهای ترانه دیوساکهه و هنگام

آغاز ترانه اتنک پس وقت انتها ترانه اساوری بست

و وقت انتها ترانه اسش هنگام آغاز نغمه پت منجری

و وقت نغمه پردازی و ترانه سازی گهری بعد از انقضاء

مقدار چهار گهری شب است تا برآمدن آفتاب مقدار

دو گهری روز و هنگام نغمه بهوپالی بعد از گذشتن

مقدار دو و نیم گهری شب است تا انقضاء شش گهری

و هفت پل و وقت نغمه ولیسکار بعد از امتضاء و انقضاء

میگهه ملهار نیز گویند که اگر شنید ترکیب میباید از للت و للهها وبی

و بهیرو و بنجم و پوربا فصل دویم در بیان آمیزها و راگنیها

غمگین بود و هندوستان مخفی مباد و محجب نمانا د

که راگنی اول راک بهیرو که نام آن بهیر معیت مرکب میکرد و از

دیلسکار و بهیرو و کنده از زورایچه توری و راگنی دوم راک بهیرو

که نامش آبهیرست از ترکیب بینه چهار است یکی تونکی

و دوم سیام و سیوم ملهار چهارم رامکلی و راگنی

سیوم راک بهیرو که نامش مده ماد هو لیست مرکب میکرد و

از اسانوری و پنجم و سیندوی و راگنی چهارم راک بهیرو

که نامش بسنت ویست مرکب میشود از اسانوری و سوره

و راگنی پنجم راک بهیرو که نامش بنگالیست صورت ترکیب

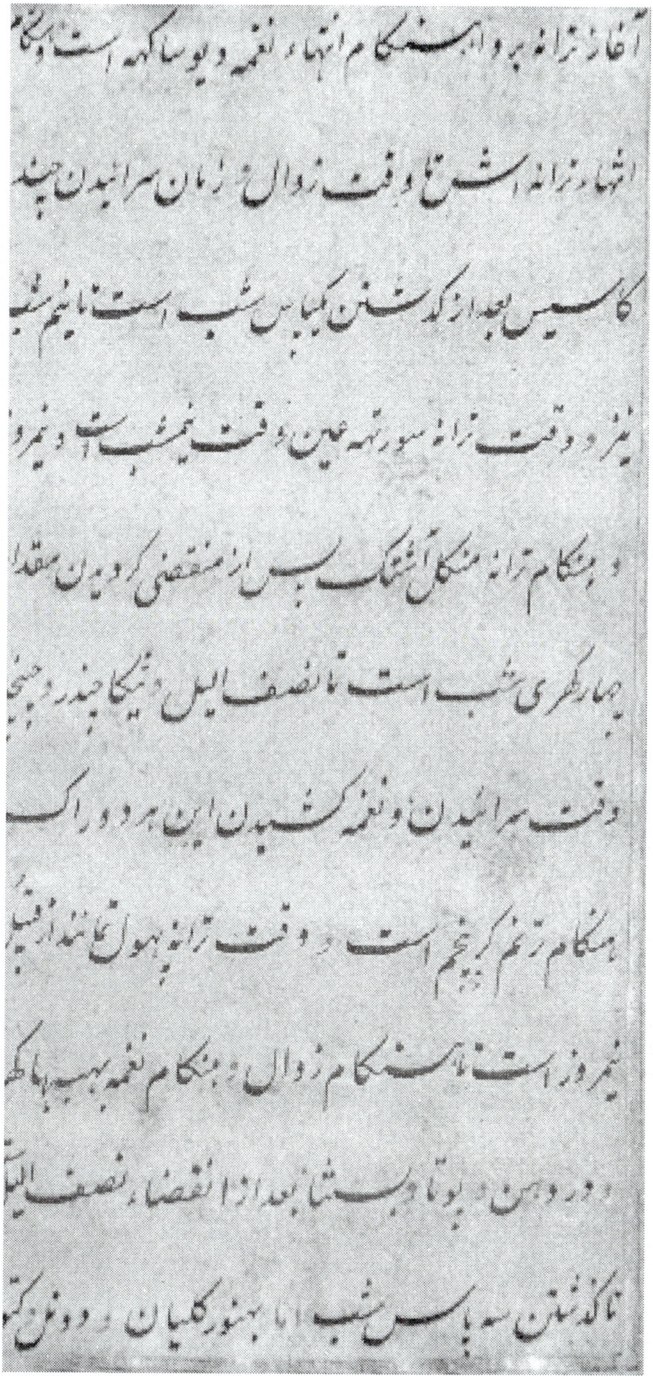

آغاز ترانه پرواهی هنگام انتهاء نغمه دیوساکهه است و هنگام

انتهاء ترانه است تا وقت زوال و زمان سرائیدن چند

کاسیس بعد از گذشتن یکپاس شب است تا نیم شب

نیز و وقت ترانه سورتهه عین وقت نیم شب است و نیز و

و هنگام ترانه منکل اشتک پس از منقضی گردیدن مقدار

چهار گهری شب است تا نصف اللیل و تیکا چندر و چنچ

وقت سرائیدن و نغمه کشیدن این هر دو راک

هنگام ترنم گرینچم است و وقت ترانه بهون کامند از قبیل

نیم روز است تا هنگام زوال و هنگام نغمه بهیه باکهه

و در وهن و بوتا وبستا بعد از انقضاء نصف اللیل

تا گذشتن سه پاس شب اما بهنور کلیان و دو نیز کیه

وکرم هنگام نغمه این همه بعد از گذشتن دو گهری

شب است تا انقضای ربع اللیل و وقت سراییدن

رام و بجکت هنگام نغمه بهول تمانند اتی و میدارد و لیکن

قبلیت مفقود است و هنگام نغمه کامود و نات و بهیهاگر

متحد است و وقت ترانه هما الا از آغاز صبح صادق تا

منقضی گردیدن مقدار چهار گهری روز است اما هنگام

نغمه مالی گورا ایس وقتیست که مقدار نیم پاس و دو گهری

از روز باقیمانده باشد تا هنگام غروب مهر و وقت سارنگا

و بجکت واحد است و وقت ترانه سوزنگ نصف

اللیل است و هنگام نغمه دیوگندهار بعد از گذشتن مقدار

دو نیم پاس و دو گهری شب تا وقتی که آفتاب جهانتاب

قدر دو گهری روز بر آمده باشد و هنگام ترانه سری تنک

بعد از انقضاء دو انقضاء سه پاس روز است تا وقت غروب

و باور گویند وقت گانرا میدارد گماسیانی و هنگام ترانه

تک بهت تونک نصف النهار است یعنی نیمروز و آخیر آن منحصر

هنگام بنگال است اما هنگام آغاز نغمه گانرا و چند گا

واحد است گمانر و هنگام انتهاء ترانه آنش وقت که

قدر یک گهری از نصف اللیل متجاوز گردد و دهرپت

و جلندهر نیز وقت بنگال میدارند و هنگام نغمه کدارا بعد از

منقضی گردیدن یک و نیم پاس روز است تا هنگام گذشتن

سه پاس و نزد بعضی از یک و نیم پاس است تا دو و نیم پاس

و یک گهری که هر وقت گانرا میدارد اما هنگام نغمه

سوم شب و یک طرف روز تا بعد از انقضای شش گهری

روز است تا انقضاء یک نیم پاس که ابتدا هنگام نغمه

کدار است و هنگام ترانه سنکرابرن و بهیباکهر متحد است

اما هنگام نغمه بلاول بعد از انقضاء نصف اللیل تا انقضاء

سه پاس شب و بسنت پنجم و للت لیکون انتهای شب

و ساکهان وقت اسا نوری میدارند و هنگام نغمه

سارنگ قبل از نیم روز مقدار دو گهری تا هنگام زوال است

و هنگام ترانه ملهار نزد بعضی وقت نغمه تنک بهالوک است

هنگام نزد بعضی بعد از گذشتن یک پاس روز تا سه پاس

و نزد بعضی به هنگام ابر و وقت ترانه کلیان بعد از گذشتن

قدر یک گهری شب است تا انقضاء شش گهری و نیم لیل

و بهاک وقت پشینه سورتهه وارد و کهنماج و کدارا

متحد الوقت اند و هنگام ترانه هیچ از نصف اللیل تا نیم پاس

شب است و وقت نغمه ججونتی از یک و نیم پاس شب است

تا هنگامی که مقدار یک پاس و دو گهری از شب باقی ماند

و سورتهه و بکهیا وقت ججونتی وارند و هنگام ترانه بنهیا

از طلوع آفتاب است تا بر آمدن دو گهری روز و هنگام

نغمه بهیهاس بعد از گذشتن مقدار سه پاس شب است

تا طلوع آفتاب و دیسکار وقت بهیهاس وارد و الله اعلم

بالصواب و الیه المرجع و المآب و برآرای مهر انجلای اولی

الالباب و بانت الکتاب خلان الصفا منبع مهر و فا

محجوب نماناد که از انجا که نکات از اقوال محال بی تامل مختلفه غیر متمسک

و ترتیب تعیین اوقات نغمات اسامی بقیه آثار موجب تث افز

می نمود و لاچار این خاکسار رنیازه آثار و سرا پا انکسار عجز شعار

با وجه بجائی الکتفاء محض شعار درزاویه بیستی واشته و بر طر

کذاشته طریق عمیق اختصار و اقتصار از اوقات نغمات

شهرت شعار انظار مذکوره مشهوره نمود و لهذا التماس

اساس میدارد که بخشش نخواهند فرمود و حمل بر نسیان

نخواهند نمود و ابواب اعتراض و اعراض نخواهند کشود

باب ششم در بیان آمیزهائی و ملونهاء راگها و راگنیها

دو در بیان تعریف آنها و درین باب پنج فصل است فصل

اول در بیان آمیزهاء راگهای شسته فصل دوم در بیان

آمیزهاء راگنیها ننگشین فصل سیوم در بیان آمیزهای

بنون راگهای بسته فصل چهارم در بیان آمیزها بعض تمامل

منسوبه بسنون موصوفه وزوجات فصل پنجم در بیان آمیزها

بعض اقسام فصل اول در بیان آمیزها یعنی ملونها

راگهای بسته بر الواح ضمایر مهر نظایر منازل شناسان

مراحل طرق موسیقی منقوش باد که چون راگهای و راگنیها

عبارت از انواع اصوات مثلثه باختصاص نشانات

بودند و از تبیین تراکیب معبر لها تعینات تراکیب

مالیعبر منها متصور می نمودند لهذا این قاصر بیان و بیان

صحت اسالیب بتکاثر اضافات مالیعبر منها بسوی معبر لها

نمی پردازد و از اکثار اقتصار مستحسن تصور دیده و از تکاثر

تا فرو زیده تراکیب مذکوره باسامی معبر لهامی آغاز ذکر جائی

که هیئت مخصوصه بتمامه مطلوب نباشد برائحه و شائبه ش

معتبر میسازد و بیت اگر گفته من گوش هوش را داری

بگویمت سخن ای آشنای بازاری ۔ دیگر راگ بهیرومین

قَطْعُ النَّظَرِ اِلَی قِیْمَتِهِ الْمُعْرَا کَمَا مَرَّ فِی بَابِ التَّقْسِیْمِ

لِاَنَّهُ یُقَالُ فِی الْهِنْدِیَّةِ سُدْه یعنی بلا آمیز مرکب میکردد

از بهاری و دیگ هاری و للیت و از هر واحد با ترکیب بهار اگر

یعنی اندک سر مطلوب است و راگ مالکوس مرکب

میشود از پرچیا و بهاری و هندول و هندول ترکیب داده

شده است آنرا از بسنت و پوربی و کلیان و کمود دیگ

مرکب میکردد از لاچوتی و سوربی و اکن جوقی و سریراگ

مرکب میشود از گوری و تهنکت و بهرش میکهه که این را بعضی

میگهه بهار نیز گویند که از سه نغمه ترکیب می‌یابد از للت و بلهاس و

و بهیرو و پنجم و پوریا فصل دویم در بیان آمیزهای راگنیهای

ششگانه بهیرو و ستان هند و ستان مخفی مباد و محجوب نماند

که راگنی اول راگ بهیرو که نام آن بهیرویست مرکب میگردد و از

دیسکار و بهیرو و گندهار و راگنه توری و راگنی دوم راگ بهیرو

که نامش آبهیریست تا مرکب شده بهار است یکی ستوکی

دوم سیام و سیوم بلهار چهارم رامکلی و راگنی

سیوم راگ بهیرو که نامش مدهماد است مرکب میگردد

از اساوری و پنجم و سیندوی و راگنی چهارم راگ بهیرو

که نامش سبندویست مرکب میشود از اساوری و سوره

و راگنی پنجم راگ بهیرو که نامش بنگالیست صورت ترکیبش

لهونه چند است یکی از بهابر است و دوم گوری و سیوم
گوجری اما توری که راگنی اول از پنج راگنیهای مالکوس است
پس مرکب میگردد از للت و دهناسری و دهولسری و سد
و سیام و بهیرو و بهیروی و راگنی دوم مالکوس که نامش
دهناسری است مرکب میشود از بهیراوی و دیوساکهه و بهیم
و این راگنی بغیر تقیید حسینی است که آن راگنی چهارم سری راگ است
کنامرو سیانی و راگنی سیوم راگ مالکوس که نامش
دهولسری است مرکب میگردد از بهیراری و جیت سری
و راگنی چهارم راگ مالکوس که نامش کنکلی است مرکب
میشود از کون و اوانا و راگنی پنجم راگ مالکوس که نامش
کهنبهاوتی است مرکب میگردد از چکاری و کهنماج و راگنیه

ملهار و اما پنج راگنیها راگ هندول پس رامکلی که راگنی اول

از انهاست مرکب میکردد از بهیم پلاسری و للت دراگنی

دوم هندول که نامش دیوساکهه است مرکب میشود

از سنکرابرن و کانرا و ملهار و راگنی سیوم هندول

که نامش للت است مرکب میکردد از سه چیز گی بهاس

و دیم و یسی سیوم راگه پنجم و راگنی چهارم هندول که نامش

بلاولی است مرکب میکردد از کهودی و کلیان و نتایئه

بلاول و راگنی پنجم راگ هندول که نامش بیت منجری است

بر دو نوعست یکی از ان بانشیفی است و دویم نامکی سه نوع

اول مرکب میکردد از پوربی و پوربا جهاکن و دهناسری

و گوری و نوع ثانی ازمار و دو هول سری و دهناسری

و کهبی و اینجا نوع اول مطلوب است پنج راگنیهاء راگ دیپک
که نام راگنی اول ازانها ویسی است پس آمیزهایش چهار اند
یکی ازانها دهول است و دوم کورا و سیوم تودی
و چهارم کهت و برای راگنی دوم راگ دیپک که نامش
کاموهنی است آمیزهایش واندکی سکهری کانرا
و دوم سورتهه و کاموی که راگنی سیوم راگ دیپک است
مرکب میشود از نت و کلیان و ملهار و راگنی چهارم
راگ دیپک که نامش کدار است آمیزهایش سه اند
یکی ازانها سنکیت و دوم سیام و سیوم مالسری
و راگنی پنجم راگ دیپک که نامش نت است و بعضی
نت نارائن نیز میگویند مرکب میشود از چهار چیز یکی ازانها

لنکدهن است دویم مدهمادهوی و سیوم بلاول

و چهارم سنکرابرن و اما پنج راگنیها سرراگ که نام راگنی

اول از انها مالسری است پس بلونیهایش چهار اند

یکی از انها مدهمادهوی است دویم سنفرستی سیوم

کدارا چهارم سنکرابرن و راگنی دوم سری راگ که

نامش بارو است مرکب بیمنو و از نبهاکی و جگت پرچیا

و شتو وا و سیام و راگنی سیوم سرراگ که نامش

گورلیست چهار آمیز نامیدارد یکی از انها پوربی است دویم

پرمنس سیوم بهاری چهارم جیتی و راگنی چهارم سرراگ

که نامش دهناسری حسینی است سوای وهناسری

فقط کمامر مرکب میکرد و از کهت و دبستی و بهیمی

بنگالیست آمیزشش پنج اند یکی از انها کانراست دوم

کهنباج وسیوم سیام وچهارم بهیرو وپنجم لبستی وپسر

پنجم راگ بهیرو که نامش ۱۰ است مرکب میگردد واز

مانجهک بهیرو وششم پسر بهیرو که نامش مادهو است

آمیزشش سه اند یکی از انها کانراست ودوم سیام وسیوم

بهیرو وپسر هفتم بهیرو که نامش کرنا ماویست ترکیبش از

از آنکه بلاول وللتی وبهیرو وهشتم پسر راگ بهیرو

که نامش منگلا بلاولست آمیزشش سه اند یکی از انها دیک

اندهارست ودوم بلاول وسیوم بهیرو واما هشتم پسر راگ

مالکونس که نام اول ازانها ویراگ نارواست پس آمیزشش

سه اند یکی از انها بسج است ودوم گداری وسیوم مالکونس

و آمیزها. پسر دوم راگ مالکوس که نامش سیووه است نیز سه اند
یکی از آنها بهاره است و دوم ملهار و سیوم مالکوس
و آمیزهای سهی مشترک که پسر سیوم مالکوس است
دو اند یکی نوقناه و دوم مالکوس و پسر چهارم مالکوس
که نامش بروا است ملونهایش پنج اند یکی از آنها بیلوست
و دوم دهناسری و سیوم رانگه توری و چهارم بهاوی
و پنجم رانگه مالکوس و ملونهای پسر پنجم مالکوس که نامش
چندرکاسیس است و دو اند یکی ایمنی و دوم مالکوس
و ملونهای سورته که ششم پسر مالکوس است چهار اند
یکی از آنها بهنس است و دوم سورته و سیوم سارنگ
و چهارم مالکوس و ملونهای راج بهرمرا که پسر هفتم مالکوس است

در ترتیب تعیین اوقات نغمات اسامی بقیه اشار موجب تشتت فر

می نمود لاچار این خاکسار نیاز آثار و سراپا انکسار عجز شعار

بوده بجای انکسار محض شعار در زاویه نیستی نشسته و برطرف

گذاشته طریق تعیین اختصار و اقتصار اوقات نغمات

شهرت شعار اشعار مذکوره مشهوره نمود لهذا التماس نیاز

اساس میدارد که رنجش نخواهند فرمود و حمل بر نسیانی

نخواهند نمود و ابواب اعتراض و اعراض نخواهند کشود

باب هفتم در بیان آمیزهائی و نام نهادن راگها و راگنیها

و در بیان تعری انها و درین باب پنج فصل است فصل

اول در بیان آمیزهاء راگهای ستة فصل دوم در بیان

آمیزهاء راگنیها رنگین فصل سیوم در بیان آمیزهائی

دو اند یکی بهیرا دوم مالکونس و ملو نهها ء هند اکه پسر هشتم

مالکونس است نیز دو اند یکی چیت و دویم مالکونس اما

هشت پسر راگ هندول که نام اول از انها منگل آشنگ است

پس آمیزها بشش ستة اند یکی از انها مالسری است و دویم

کانرا و سیوم کلیان چهارم سیام پنجم کدارا و ششم

هندول و آمیزها ء تیکا چند که پسر دویم مالکونس است سه اند

یکی از انها للت است بسکون الثانی و دویم ملهار و سیوم

هندول و آمیزهای بسنجل که پسر سیوم راگ هندول است

چهار اند یکی از انها بهیر سیت و دویم بلاول و سیوم بسنت

و چهارم هندول و آمیزها ء بهول تمانند که پسر چهارم هندول است

سه اند یکی سارنگی دویم ملهاری و سیوم هندول و آمیزهای

بهت بهاگهر که پسر پنجم راگ هندول است چهار اندکی سنگرا

دویم دیبکی سیوم بلاول چهارم هندول در آمیزها پسر

ششم راگ هندول که نامش وروهن است سه اندکی کسلبنی

دویم ناکر سیوم هندول در آمیزها پوناکه هفتم پسر هندول است

نیز سه اندکی منگلی دویم کانرا سیوم هندول در آمیزهائی

بسنت هشتم راگ هندول که نامش بسنت است چهار اندکی

یکی از انها کانرا است دویم بسنت سیوم راگیه بهیرو

چهارم هندول دو واضح باد که در آمیزها تمامی پسرهای

هندول مراد از نوکر هندول انچه اوست نه بهشت و نکی مثه

اما هشت پسر راگ دیپک که نام پسر اول از انها هنوز

کلیان است پس آمیزهایش چهار اندکی مارواد دویم کلیان

سیوم جیتی و چهارم بهیاس و آمیزها دونل که پسر

دویم و بیبک است دو اند و جیبکی و دو هناسری و آمیزها

رام که پسر سیوم و بیبک است نیز دو اندکی بهنسی

و دوم سارنگ و چهارم پسر و بیبک که نامش کنولاست

مرکب بسیار دواز کانرا و للتی و آمیزها کرم که پسر پنجم و بیبک است

سه اندکی ملاول و دیم ایمن سیوم هنبری و آمیزهای تجکیب

که پسر ششم و بیبک است پنج اندکی و هناسری و دوم سوزهه

سیوم برهنش چهارم بسنت پنجم بنگلا و آمیزها کامود

که پسر هفتم و بیبک است سه اندکی سورتهه و دوم کانرا سیوم

کامود و آمیزها همالا که پسر هشتم و بیبک است دو اندکی بهار

دوم و بیبک و معلوم باد که و بیبک و و بیبک الله نارز اک و احاست

ونزد بعضی دو اند اما هشت پسر سری راگ که نام پسر اول

از انهامالی گوره است پس بهونهایش بسته اند یکی از انها

بهیروست دوم نت وسیوم کلیان چهارم ملهار پنجم

دیک اند ششم گوری و آمیزهاء سارنگا که پسر دوم سری راگ است

سه اند یکی از انها سده سارنگ دوم برنس سارنگ

سیوم سورتهه و آمیزهاء سونرنگ که پسر سیوم سری راگ است

دو اند یکی بسونا دوم ملهار و آمیزهاء دیوگندهار که پسر چهارم سری راگ

است چهار اند یکی از انها آسی است دوم دهول سیوم

بهیرو چهارم سارنگ و پنجم پسر سری راگ که نامش نت

نک است آمیزهایش دو اند یکی گوری دوم جیت و این

راگ افضل از برادران است در حین سماع و آمیزهاء با دیرگونه

و بهاک وقت پیشینه سورتهه وارد و کهنماج و کدارا
متحد الوقت اند و هنگام ترانه بهج از نصف اللیل تا نیم پاس
شب است و وقت نغمه ججونتی از یک و نیم پاس شب است
تا هنگامی که مقدار یک پاس و دو گهری از شب باقی ماند
و سورتهه و بکهیا وقت ججونتی دارند و هنگام ترانه بهیا
از طلوع آفتاب است تا بر آمدن دو گهری روز و هنگام
نغمه بهبهاس بعد از گذشتن مقدار سه پاس شب است
تا طلوع آفتاب و بیسکار وقت بهبهاس دارد و الله اعلم
بالصواب و الیه المرجع و المآب دیباره مهر انجلای اولی
الالباب و بانت الکتاب خلان الصفا منبع مهر و فا
محجوب نماناد که از انجا که بنگارش اقوال مجال بی‌تال مختلفه غیر متمسکه

که پسر ششم سری راگ است نیز دو اند یکی ایشان دوم ملهار آمیزهاء

نک بهانوک که پسر هفتم سری راگ است ایضا دو اند یکی بروا دوم

ململی و آمیزهاء آهیرا که پسر هشتم سری راگ است چهار اند یکی

نت دوم بلاول سیوم گوند ملهار چهارم کهنباج والا هشت

پسر میگهه که نام پسر اول از انها کانرا است پس آمیزهاء ایش

سه اند یکی کالیکهه دوم ملهار سیوم بلاول و آمیزهاء [illegible]

که پسر دوم میگهه است هم سه اند یکی از انها کامود دوم

نت سیوم سیام و آمیزهاء کدارا که پسر سیوم میگهه است

چهار اند یکی از انها [illegible] است دوم هندول سیوم [illegible]

چهارم رانجه بهاک و آمیزهای جلندهر که پسر چهارم میگهه است

سه اند یکی نت دوم سیام سیوم سورتهه و [illegible]

نیز دهر که پسر پنجم میکهه است چهار اند یکی از انها

غار است دوم گوند سیوم ملهار چهارم بسنت و آمیزها

سوهب که ششم پسر میکهه است دو اند یکی سکهری

دوم ملهار و آمیزها یک هر نوناکه پسر هفتم میکهه است سه اند

یکی از انها توریت دوم للت بفتح الاول و سکون الثانی

سیوم بسنت و آمیزها سنکرابرن که ششم پسر

میکهه است سته اند یکی از انها مالسری است دوم کدارا

سیوم بسنت چهارم سیام پنجم بهاکی ششم کنوس پس بالله

انّه یعلم بحقیقة الحال و منه التوفیق وطاقة المقال

فصل چهارم در بیان آمیزها بعض نهاسل منسوبه بنون

موصوفه وز وجات بر رای ویانت اثنای ارباب رکاوت

انشعاب مشروح باو کرآمیز باد بسنت پنجم بسته اند یکی از

انها بسنتی کانراست دوم کداری سیوم بهار چهارم

کنوس سس پنجم للت ششم بهیرو و توتز و بعض از استادان

و ماهران این فن بسنت پنجم مرکب میکرد و از ساز نگ و نت

و ملهار دراگنه بلاول و دیوکری و بهیرو و اما در عوام الناس

شهرت آمیزایش ت بنج راگنی گردیده است و این سخن

تحقیق نرسیده است و ملونیهای پوریا و اندیکی پوربی

دوم بهاک و بهاکرا مرکب میکرد و از سه چیز یکی از انها

کدارا است دوم کوری سیوم سام و ملونیهای گنهاج دو انها

یکی مالسری دوم ملهار و ملونیهای بهپالس سه اند یکی تار و ا

دوم رامی سیوم بهو پالی و سا و بنک مرکب میکرد

انپنج چیز یکی از انها نت است دوم کدارا سیوم کانرا

چهارم کاموو پنجم سیام و ملونهای ملهار سه اند یکی نت

دوم سارنگ سیوم میکهه و ملونهای ولیکار پنج اند

یکی از انها کوری است دوم مارو سیوم دهولسری

چهارم جیت سری پنجم دهناسری و ملونهای ایمن سه اند

یکی کلیان دوم کدارا سیوم بلاول و ملونهای دیوکری

دو اند یکی شده سارنگ دوم پوربی و ملونهای برهنس

نیز دو اند یکی گوری دوم بهیبهاس و ملونهای سارنگ

چهار اند یکی از انها دیوگری است دوم ملهار سیوم نت

چهارم سده نت و ملونهای هنبر چهار اند یکی دیسکی

دوم کلیان سیوم گوجری چهارم سیام و گلب راک

مرکب میشود از بلاول و پوربی و کدارا و دیوگری و مده مادهو

و آمیزهاء و یک انهار چهار اند یکی گوری دویم سده سانوری

سیوم سارنگ چهارم بهیرو و ملونهای گوراسه اند یکی

گوری دویم نت سیوم بهیرو و ملونهائی سوها دو اند یکی سده

بلاول دویم کیسری و ملونهای لنک و بن نیز دو اند یکی بهاری

دویم کدارا و ملونهائی کهت راک سه اند یکی از انجا

اسانوریست دویم توری سیوم سیام چهارم الوا

پنجم گنده‌ها ششم پیراری و ملونهاء دیس کلاسه اند یکی از انها

دیسی است دویم توری سیوم للت و ملونهاء جونراشتک

چهار اند یکی آسانوری دویم پوربی سیوم بهیرو چهارم

دیوکندهار و ملونهای ناک سوها سه اند یکی سوها دویم ملهار

سیوم کدارا و ملونیهای سراج بهیرس دو اند یکی آن سبراک

دوم مالوا و ملونیهای کلاهس سه اند یکی از انها کلیان است

دوم بهاکرا سیوم کانرا و ملونیهای جیز بهیلا چهار اند یکی از انها

رامکلی است دوم گوجری سیوم ولیکان چهارم بسنت

و ملونیهای سنکگرمن سه اند یکی از انها للت دیمن دوم

سورتهه سیوم بلاول و ملونیهای بیراتی نیز سه اند یکی از انها

ولسکار است دوم توری سیوم تروت و ملونیهای کورکلی

دو اند یکی گجری دوم اسا توری و در ملونیهای توناتت اختلاف

واقع است گاهی مرکب میکرد و از کلیان و نت و گاهی

از کانرا و نت و گاهی از کامود و نت و گاهی از سارنگ

و نت و بسنت و بیراتی مرکب میکرد و از همه جیز یکی از انها

دیوگری است دویم پوربی سیوم گوری و ملونهای پوربی

نیز سه اند یکی جوگیا دویم رانجه دیوگری است سیوم پوربا

و آمیزهای پوربا دو اند دهوسری و گازا سده و ملونهای

بهیم سه اند دهناسری و بروا و گازا و آمیزهای نرمن که ازرا

نردون نیز میگویند و نزد بعضی هردو راگ متغایرند چهار اند

یکی ازانها مارو است دویم گوری سیوم رانجه دهناسری

چهارم شائبه کورا و ملونهای جیتی کوری هم چهار اند

یکی مالکوس دویم مارو است سیوم شائبه پوربا چهارم گوری

و ملونهای مارو سه اند یکی بهاس دویم شائبه گوری و سیوم

مارو و هویدا باد که چون از محققین و مدققین مهتار

ذوی الاعتبار شناوران ابحار موسیقی آمیزهای این قدر

اسامی از شاخسار مذکوره بتحقیق در رسیده این سراپا

افتقار لاچار برین مقدار اکتفا درزید و بتوفیق که دوستان

ذوالکمال خیال محال اهمال بنال بخواهند گذرانید و از کشش

نصال نهال طبعیت را بر سر آتاج فروتنی نخواهند بارانید

فصل پنجم دربیان آمیزها بعض اقسام و وجه

البعضیة انه لا ترکیب له فی الاقسام الذی

سمیت باسده فافهم و تدبر برافکار انوار اشعار

بلغای فراست اساس و وجدان ضمیر مهر نظیر حکمای

حقیقت شناس مکشوف باد و مخفی نماند که از چهار قسم

راگ بهیرو که نام قسم اول از انها بهیرو سده است و آمیز

ندارد و آمیزهای هر واحد قسم ثانی و ثالث و رابعش دو دو

اما آن دو ملونی که برای قسم ثانی مقرر اند یکی از آنها سنکرنی
است دوم بهیرو و ملونهای قسم ثالث بهیرو و کرلاوتی
معین نموده اند و ملونهای قسم رابع بهیرو و آنچه للت
بسکون الثانی است و آمیزهای غنچه بهیرو شده که نامش
کن کلی است سه اند یکی دیگ انداز دوم بهیرو و سیوم
بسنتی و ملونهای غنچه کیزی که نامش اسکلی مذکور کرده
نیز سه اند یکی از آنها لجری است دوم ویسی توری سیوم
بهیرو و ملونهای غنچه سکیا سکهیرن که نامش برکاس کلی است
نیز دو اند یکی لاول و دوم بهیرو و اما نه اقسام توری بدون
توری سده پس ملونهای قسم اول از آنها که نامش
توری بهرار است سه اند یکی از آنها ویسکار است دوم تردن

که بعیث مخصوص صحبت سامعه مطلوب نباشد بالحنه و شائبه

معیر سیار و بیت اگر گفته من گوش هوش را داری

بگو بیت سخن ای آشنائی بزاری اگر راگ بهیرو مین

قَطَعُ النَّظَرِ اِلَی قِسْمِیهِ المُعَرّا کَمَا مَرَّ فِی بَابِ التَّقْسِیم

لِاَنَّهُ یُقَالُ فِی الهِنْدِیَة سُدّه یعنی بلا آمیز مرکب میگردد

از بهاری و دیکی هاری و للت و از هر واحد تا بترکیب بهار ایکم

یعنی اندک سر مطلوب است و راگ مالکوس مرکب

میشود از پرچیا و بهاری و هندول و هندول ترکیب داده

شده است آنرا از بسنت و پوربی و کلیان و کمود و دیگ

مرکب میگردد از لانچوتی و سوربی و اگن جوتی و سرراگ

مرکب میشود از گوری و دهنک و برانی و میگهه که این را بعضی

بنون راگهای ستة فصل چهارم در بیان آمیزها بعض تأمل

منسوبه بسنون موصوفه وز وجات فصل پنجم در بیان آمیزها

بعض اقسام فصل اول در بیان آمیزها یعنی لمونهای

راگهای ستة بر الواح ضمائر مهر نظائر منازل شناسان

مراحل طرق موسیقی منقوش باد که چون راگهای و راگنیهای

عبارت از انواع اصوات مؤلفه باختصاص نسبات

بودند و از ترکیب بین تراکیب معبر لها تعینات تراکیب

ما یعبر منها متصور می نمودند لهذا این قاصر بیان در بیان

صحت اسالیب مبتکر اضافات ما یعبر منها بسوی معبر لها

نمی پردازد و از اکثار اقتصار مستحسن تصور دیده و از تکرار

تا فروزیده تراکیب مذکوره باسامی معبر لها می آغاز ذکر جائے

سوم شب و یک گهری نو ثو تا بعد از انقضای شش گهری

روز است تا انقضاء یک و نیم پاس که ابتداء هنگام نغمه

کدار است و هنگام ترانه سنکرابرن و بهیاکهر متحد است

اما هنگام نغمه بلاول بعد از انقضاء نصف اللیل تا انقضاء

سه پاس شب و بسنت پنجم و للت بسکون الثانی

و ساکهان وقت اسا نوری میدارند و هنگام نغمه

سارنگ قبل از نیم روز مقدار دو گهری تا هنگام زوال است

و هنگام ترانه ملهار نیز و بعضی وقت نغمه تک بهالوک است

گمان روز و بعضی بعد از گذشتن یکپاس روز تا سه پاس

روز و بعضی هنگام ابر و وقت ترانه کلیان بعد از گذشتن

قدر یک گهری شب است تا انقضاء شش گهری و سه پل

سوم شب و یک پهر بود تا بعد از انقضای شش گهری

روز است تا انقضاء یک و نیم پاس که ابتداء هنگام نغمه

کدار است و هنگام ترانه سنکرابرن و بهباگهر متحد است

اما هنگام نغمه بلاول بعد از انقضاء نصف اللیل تا انقضاء

سه پاس شب و بسنت پنجم و للت لیکون الثانیه

و ساکهان وقت اسا نوری میدارند و هنگام نغمه

سارنک قبیل از نیم روز مقدار دو گهری تا هنگام زوال است

و هنگام ترانه ملهار نیز و بعضی وقت نغمه تک بهالوک است

هنگام روز و بعضی بعد از گذشتن یک پاس روز تا سه پاس

روز و بعضی هنگام ابر و وقت ترانه کلیان بعد از گذشتن

قدر یک گهری شب است تا انقضاء شش گهری و سه پل

سیوم توری و ملونیهای قسم ثانی که نامش توری بهادریست

نیز سه اند یکی توری دوم رانکه سری سیوم شتابه و لیساولی

و ملونیهای قسم ثالث که نامش توری دیسی است

اساوری و توری ورانکه لاچاریست و ملونیهای قسم رابع

که نامش توری جونپوریست بزو او توری و رانکه

ملبار رمعین ساخته اند و ملونیهای قسم خامس که نامش توری

اسانوریست دو اند یکی اسانوری دوم توری و ملونیهای

قسم سادس که نامش توری منکلیکهه است سه اند

یکی سکهری دوم توری سیوم رانکه صدای فرحت انتماء

بلاول و ملونیهای قسم سابع که نامش توری لاچاریست

چهار اند یکی ازانها دهناسریست دوم ویسی سیوم حسینی

اِسْمُ کُلِّ واحِدٍ مِنَ الْمُرَکَّبِ مِنْ تَسْمِیَةِ الْمُرَکَّبِ

بهی یکی نت است دویم ماهار و ملونهای قسم رابع که

نامش نت نارائن است چهار اند یکی نت دویم ملهار سیوم

بلاول چهارم اوانا و ملونهای قسم خامس که نامش نت

آهیر است نیز چهار اند یکی نت دویم بلاول سیوم سورتهه چهارم

بهاک و ملونهای قسم سادس که نامش نت نارو است دو اند

یکی نت دویم نارو و ملونهای قسم سابع که نامش نت اسانوری است

سه اند یکی سکهری دویم ملهار سیوم نت و اما چهار اقسام مالسری

که قسم اول از انها سری سده است کما مرّ و علمت فی باب التقسیم

پس ملونهای قسم ثانی که نامش جیت سری است سه اند یکی جیت

دویم دهناسری سیوم رالکه کوری ملونهای قسم ثالث که نامش

پرناپ سری است نیز سه اند یکی سیام دوم کوری سیوم

دنهاسری و ملونیهای قسم رابع که وهو لسریٹ

واما دو قسم

کوری که یک قسم از انها کوری سده است پس ملونیهای قسم ثانی

که نامش جینتی کوری است چهار اند یکی از انها ماکونس است

دویم مارو اسیوم رانگه بوریا چهارم کوری واما سه قسم اسانوری

که نام قسم اولش اسانوری سده است پس ملونیهائی قسم ثانی

که نامش اسانوری جوکیا است پنج اند یکی جوکاوتی دوم اسانوری

سیوم رانگه توری چهارم آسکندی پنجم دیسی و ملونیهائی قسم

ثالث که نامش اسانوری صورتخان است سه اند یکی اسانوری

دوم بروا سیوم رانگه توری واما سه اقسام کجری

که نام قسم اول از انها گجری سده است و آمیزنا مند از دو پیش

ملونهای قسم ثانی که نامش کهت گجری است سه اند یکی کهت

دوم رامکلی سیوم گجری و ملونهای قسم ثالث که نامش

سیام گجریست نیز سه اند یکی گجری دوم سیام سیوم

رانجه بلاول و اما چهارده اقسام بلاول که نام قسم اولش

بلاول سده مقرر نموده اند کهامر پس ملونهای قسم ثانی

که نامش بلاول گکب است پنج اند یکی رانجه مالسری دوم

ست بهبه چوهی سیوم بلاول چهارم بهاک پنجم صند وریه

و آمیزهای قسم ثالث که نامش بلاول سکل تحریر یافته و آنها

یکی کوند دوم نت ونزو بعضی سه اند بمعاقب بلاول

و آمیزهای قسم رابع که نامش بلاول الهیا است چهار اند

یکی از آنها بلاول است دویم راگنی بهاگ سیوم بهو پالی
چهارم پوربا و آمیز های قسم خامس که نامش بلاول
کهماچی است و اند کما یفهم انهم کلهم واحد من هیئة
الترکیبیه یعنی کهماج و بلاول و آمیز های قسم سادس که نامش
بلاول جوجونتی است نیز دو اند یکی بلاول دویم جوجونتی و آمیز های
قسم سابع که نامش بلاول سنکرا است ایضاً تفهم من
تسمیته یعنی بلاول و سنکرا است و آمیز های قسم ثامن
که نامش بلاول کهنبایتی است عبارات و ملهار و بلاول مقرر
نموده اند و آمیز های قسم تاسع که نامش بلاول ایمن است و دو اند
یکی ایمن کلیان دویم بلاول آمیز های قسم عاشر که نامش
کاموده بلاول است و آمیز های قسم حادی عشر که نامش

دهن سکیا بلاول است تفهم من التشبیهما و نزد بعضی نام

قسم دهم ولوکری بلاول است و نام قسم یازدهم بلاول بهاکت

و ما بین کبان منه ایضا یفهم من التسمیهما و آمیزاو

قسم ثانی عشر که نامش سکیا بلاول است و اندکی کانزادوم

بهار و نزد بعضی ست اند متعاقب البلاول بالاثنین

المذکورتین و آمیزاو قسم ثالث عشر که نامش

بلاول بهاکت فقد سبق فی کره و آمیزاو قسم رابع عشر

که نامش بلاول سوهاست و اندکی بلاول و دوم سوها و نزد

بعضی سنکری و بهار نیز متعاقب میشود اما چهار قسم

للت بسکون الثانی که نام قسم اول ازانها للت بهار است

پس آمیزایش چهار اندکی برجیا و دوم بهار سوم کدار

چهارم للت و آمیزها منقسم بعضها آمیزهای للت بهار است
لیکن للت مفقود است و آمیزهای قسم ثانی که نامش
للتاکدار است دو اندکی کدارا دویم للت و آمیزهای قسم
ثالث که نامش للت مارو است نیز دو اندکی مارو دویم
للت و آمیزها قسم رابع که نامش لالیتی است
سه اندکی از آنها للت است دویم بهیرو سیوم رامکلی بهار
و اما چهار قسم ساکهه که نام قسم اولش دیو کهه است
سه اندکی اعلمت ایاها فی بعضها و نیز و بعضی چهار اندکی از آنها
اول آن آسا است دویم توری سیوم سکهری چهارم ملهار اما
این قول اصح است و آمیزها قسم ثانی که نامش کن کهه
است سه اندکی ششها دویم ملهار سیوم گوند

و آمیزهٔ قسم ثالث که نامش بهیرب کهه است نیز سه اند
یکی سکهراوی و دویم ملهاری سیوم اسانوری و آمیزهٔ
قسم رابع که نامش بهنورسا کهه است کانراو بلاول و ملهار است
و اما یازده اقسام سارنگ که نام قسم اول از انها سارنگ
سند مقرر گردید پس آمیزهٔ قسم دوم که نامش بندرای
سارنگ است چهار اند یکی سارنگ دویم بروا سیوم
رانگیه ملهار و چهارم سورتهه و آمیزهٔ قسم سیوم که
نامش گورسارنگ است سه اند یکی رانجه و دیوکری دویم
پوربا کلیان سیوم سارنگ و آمیزهٔ قسم چهارم که
نامش گورسارنگ گوپرناری است چهار اند یکی از انها سارنگ
دویم پوربا سیوم کلیان چهارم دیوکری و آمیزهٔ قسم

پنجم که نامش سارنگ نت دهات است پنج اندکی سورنهه دوم
ملهار سوم سارنگ چهارم افزانیچم برنس لیکن در
قسمین اخیرین رانجه وشابه مطلوبست و آمیزهای قسم ششم
که نامش سارنگ مس است دوانه کمابیش همین اینیه
یعنی سارنگ پنج حسس و آمیزهای قسم هفتم که نامش
مدهون سارنگ است چهار اندکی سارنگ دوم رانکه
سیوم شابه سورنهه چهارم سیهانا کانزا و آمیزهای قسم هشتم
که نامش ساونت سارنگ است سه اندکی ملهار دوم سارنگ
سیوم بلاول و آمیزهای قسم نهم که نامش دهوریا سارنگست
نیز سه اندکی للت دوم سارنگ سیوم ملهار و آمیزهای قسم دهم
که نامش دهوریا سارنگست دو اندکی سورنهه دوم سارنگ

آمیزنا قسم یازدهم که نامش سجانانکت رنگست سه اندکی کهناج دوم

ملهار سیوم سارنگ اما یازده اقسام ملهار که نام قسم اول

از انها ملهار سده منفرد گردید پس ملونهار قسم ثانی که نامش

گوند ملهار است سه اندکی آداناو دویم رانجه سوهی سیوم

ملهار و ملونهار قسم ثالث که نامش میگهه ملهار است در بحث

آمیزنا گذشت و ملونهار قسم رابع که نامش دهوریا

ملهار است پنج اندکی رانجه للت دویم کانرا شهانا

سیوم سارنگ چهارم کهناج پنجم ملهار و آمیزنا قسم خامس

که نامش ملرسون ملهار است سه اندکی آداناو دویم کهناج سیوم

ملهار و آمیزناء قسم سادس که نامش رامداسی ملهار است

بزرسه اندکی بردی سورتهه دوم جچوتی سارنگ سیوم ملهار

و آمیزهای قسم سابع که نامش سورداسی ملهار است چهار آن
یکی از آنها برهمسی است دوم ملهار سیوم راگه کانرا
چهارم شاشبه سارنگ و آمیزهای قسم ثامن که نامش ساونت
ملهار است سه اند یکی راگه برواد دوم نت سیوم
ملهار و آمیزهای قسم تاسع که نامش ساتونی ملهار است
دو اند یکی دیگ انداز دوم ملهار و آمیزهای قسم عاشر
که نامش میگهاونی ملهار است چهار اند یکی جیوتی
دوم سارنگ سیوم راگه گوند چهارم ملهار و آمیزهای
قسم حادی عشر که نامش هندولی ملهار است سه اند یکی
ملهار دوم راگه بهار سیوم راگه للت و اما چهار قسم
گور که نام قسم اولش گور اسده است کما مر فی التقسیم

پس آمیزهای قسم ثانی که نامش تالی گوراست پنج اند یکی
بهیرو دوم نت سوم ناسری چهارم شائبه دیکت اندهار
پنجم رانچه ملهار و آمیزهای قسم ثالث که نامش جهنی گوراست
دو اند یکی جیت دویم کدارا و آمیزهای قسم رابع که نامش
سری گوراست سه اند یکی گوری دویم دهناسری سیوم
رانچه تردن اما دو قسم جوک که نام قسم اولش جوک
سده است کمار لیک ملونهای قسم ثانی که نامش جوک سکلست
چهار اند یکی رانچه پوربی دویم دهول سیوم شائبه بروا
چهارم آسا و اما سه اقسام سیام که نام قسم اول از انها
سیام سج است لیک ملو نهاد قسم دویم که نامش
سیام کلیان است سه اند یکی کلیان دویم بلاول

سیوم راگنیه کدارا و آمیزها، قسم سیوم که نامش سیام کدار است

و وانی یکی سیام و دوم کدارا اما سه قسم کامود شده

که نام قسم اول از انها کامود است و در آمیزاتش اختلاف است

نزد بعضی مونهابش و وانی یکی بهار و دویم کلیان و نزد

بعضی بلاول و کامود و آمیزها، قسم ثانی که نامش تلک

کامود است نیز دو وانی یکی کهت و دوم کامود و آمیزشها،

قسم ثالث که نامش سیانوت کامود است و بعضی

بعکس الترتیب میگویند ایضا و وانی یکی کلیان و دویم کامود

و اما سیزده اقسام کلیان که نام قسم اول از انها شده کلیان است

پس آمیزها، قسم ثانی که نامش ایمن کلیان است

چهار انه یکی از انها راگنه بلاول است و دویم راگنه پوربا سیوم

کلیان و چهارم دهول و آمیزهای قسم ثالث که نامش
یمن کلیان است سه اند یکی پوربی دوم بهاک سیوم کانرا
غارا و ملونیهای قسم رابع که نامش بهوپالی کلیان است
نیز سه اند یکی بهیم پلاس دوم بهاری و گرناسی نیز میگویند
و سیوم کلیان و ملونیهای قسم خامس که نامش پوریا
کلیان است پوربا و کلیان و در اسحه بهاک معین نموده اند
و آمیزهای قسم سادس که نامش شیر کلیان است سه اند
یکی شیر دوم نت سیوم بهوپالی کلیان و آمیزهای قسم سابع
که نامش سیام کلیان است دو اند یکی سیام دوم کلیان
و آمیزها قسم ثامن که نامش سانوی کلیان است پنج اند
یکی ازانها نت است دوم بهوپالی سیوم بهاک

چهارم کدارا پنجم کلیان و آمیزها قسم تاسع که نامش کاموده

کلیانست چهار اند یکی نت دویم کلیان سیوم کوند

چهارم بلاول ونیز بعضی آمیزهایش دو اند یکی کامود

دویم کلیان و آمیزها قسم عاشر که نامش نت کلیان است

نفهم من اسمه یعنی دو اند یکی نت دویم کلیان آمیزهای

قسم حادی عشر که نامش بهاک کلیان است نیز دو اند یکی

بهاک دوم کلیان و آمیزهای قسم ثانی عشر که نامش

بهیم کلیان است چهار اند یکی از انها کلیانست دویم

کامودی سیوم راگه بلاول چهارم کدارا و آمیزهای

قسم ثالث عشر که نامش کهیم کلیانست نیز چهار اند

یکی نت دویم سورتهه سیوم همیر و چهارم کلیان

و اما هژده اقسام کانڑا که نام قسم اولش کانڑا است

پس ملونهای قسم دویم که نامش نایکی کانڑا است چهار اند یکے

ملهار دویم رالجه پنج و سیوم شابه سکهراوی و چهارم کانڑا

و ملونهای قسم سیوم که نامش سهانا کانڑا است سه اند یکی رالجه

غار پنج دویم جهونج سیوم کانڑا و ملونهای قسم چهارم که نامش

اڈانا کانڑا است دو اند یکی گوند ملهار دویم کانڑا و آمیزهای قسم پنجم

که نامش سکهراوی کانڑا است سه اند یکی دیو ساکه دویم رالجه

سهانا کانڑا سیوم ملهار و آمیزهای قسم ششم که نامش اکیل

کانڑا است چهار اند یکی پردیپکی دوم جهومری سیوم کانڑا چهارم

سنهکرا و آمیزهای قسم هفتم که نامش منده کهه کانڑا است نیز چهار اند

یکی کانڑا دویم برواب سوم شابه مالکوس چهارم ملهار و آمیز

قسم هشتم که نامش کهمبیری کانر است و واند یکی کانرا دویم

مالسری و آمیز ها، قسم نهم که نامش کونیه کانر است نیز دو اند

یکی مالکوس، دویم کانرا و نزد بعضی را که کنهاج نیز داخل است

و آمیز ها، قسم دهم که نامش سنی کانر است سه اند یکی

بهار، دویم بسنت سیوم کانرا و آمیز های قسم یازدهم که

نامش کنهاچی کانر است و واند یکی کنهاج و دوم کانرا و آمیز ها

قسم دوازدهم که نامش سورتهه کانر است نیز دو اند سورتهه

و کانرا و آمیز های قسم سیزدهم که نامش جهونتی کانر است

کما تعلم من اسمه یعنی جهونتی و کانرا و آمیز های قسم

چهاردهم که نامش درباری کانر است پنج اند یکی دیوساکهه

دویم اڈانا سیوم شبانه مالکونس چهارم کانرا پنجم راکهه

نهار و آمیزها قسم پانزدهم که نامش کرناتی کانرا است

چهار اند یکی کانرا دوم بارو سیوم سورتهه چهارم لبورنبی

و آمیزها قسم شانزدهم که نامش غارا کانرا است نیز چهار اند

یکی تلنگی دوم کانرا سیوم رانجه کهماج و چهارم بها

و آمیزها قسم هفدهم که نامش سنکلیکه کانرا است و دو اند

یکی کانرا دوم رانجه چاول کلب آمیزها قسم هژدهم که نامش

دولتی کانرا است سه اند یکی مالکونس دوم و بهاسریه

سیوم کانرا اما دو قسم بهاک که نام قسم اول از آن بهاک

سده است پس مونهائی قسم ثانی که نامش بهاکر است چهار اند

یکی رانجه نت دوم شانبه چاول سیوم دیناسریه

چهارم بهاک اما پنج قسم کدارا که نام قسم اولش کدارا سده است

پس ملونهای قسم ثانی که نامش سیام کدار است دو اند
یکی سیام دوم کدار و ملونهای قسم ثالث که نامش
نت کدار است نیز دو اند نت و کدار و ملونهای قسم
رابع که نامش للتا کدار است سه اند یکی للت دوم
کدار سیوم رانجه مالکونش و ملونهای قسم خامس که
نامش مارو کدار است هم سه اند یکی مارو دویم برج و سیوم
کدارا اما چهار اقسام سنکرا که نام قسم اولش سنکرا
سد و است پس ملونهای قسم ثانی که نامش سنکهرا
بدن است و در بحث ملونهای بنون میکهه تحریر و تسطیر کرده
و ملونهای قسم ثالث که نامش سنکرا اران است
سه اند یکی سنکرا دوم کدارا سیوم و بناسری

و ملونهای قسم راج که نامش سنکراسنکبهرن است

دوازدهی سنکرا دویم پرج اما دو قسم کهناج که نام قسم

اولش کهناج سده است پس ملونها و قسم ثانی که نامش

جوگیا کهنا چست دوازدهی جوگ دوم پرج اما دو قسم

ججونتی که نام قسم اولش ججونتی است مین غیر تقیید التسمیه

بشیئ آخر پس ملونهایش چهار یکی بهنس

دوم سورتهه سیوم سارنگ چهارم ملهار و ملونهای

قسم ثانی که نامش ججونتی کانرا است در بحث ملونهای

اقسام کانرا مذکور اما دو قسم سورتهه که نام قسم اولش

سورتهه سده است پس ملونهای قسم دوم که نامش سورتهه

سارنگ است و سورتهه سارنگ نیز سکویند در بحث ملونهای اقسا

ساز نگ گفته شد و مکشوف باد هنگامی که در کتب و یا
در تب بدین ما الهار شش راگ و سی راگنی گفته شود و آنرا
راگ کر گویند و ساگری صورت مجتمعه هفت راگ گویند و آن
هفت این است بهیرو، للت، ملهار، کونر، ججونتی، سوریته،
جاول، مالکونس منه باب هشتم در بیان سازها و تالها

بر وجدان ضمائر آئینه نظائر استادان و ماهران این زمان
مکشوف گردیده باشد که سازها و آلات نغمه جمله فی الاصل دوازده اند
و تالها نوزده و دوازده و ده سازها نغمه سازها بسمع مبارک سلاطین
در رسیده و نغمه و ساز گاهی شنیده اما آن ده سازها که نغمه
آنها فرح الاسماع ظل الٰهی گردیده و بسمع شاهنشاهی در رسیده و یکی
از آنها طنبور است دویم بین سیوم رباب چهارم مردنگ

پنجم چو و ششم چیت رنگ هفتم واربا هشتم و هولک نهم پکهاوج

دهم بردی و اما آن دو ساز که بالتفات سلاطین گشته اند یکی

قانون و دوم کهنیرو و اما نالهای نوزده نام یکی از انها یکاست نام

دوم چهارتال نام پنجم دو ناله کلان نام ششم تهته نام هفتم

سونرنا حنفه نام هشتم سواری پنجتاله نام نهم چهارتاله نام و دهم سواری

بمغنت ناله نام یازدهم و چهارکه بهاکت نیز گویند نام دوازدهم کیت

سنکیت نام سیزدهم برم نازده ناله نام چهاردهم برم ناله

نام پانزدهم و هواشانزدهم ناتها هفدهم رودنگ هژدهم و دایان

نوزدهم فردوست